GW00503094

Ups and Downs of My Life

Ups and Downs of My Life

++++++++++++++++++++++++

Always Trying to Be Positive

Veronica Orsborn

Copyright © 2023 by Veronica Orsborn

All rights reserved. No part of this book may be reproduced or used in any manner
without written permission of the copyright owner except for the use of quotations in
a book review. For more information, contact: veronica.mcbean@hotmail.co.uk

First paperback edition 2023

978-1-80541-028-7 (paperback)
978-1-80541-029-4 (ebook)

Dedicated to my son, Trevor David Barnes,
who has always been there for me.

Contents

Book One

MY CHILDHOOD DAYS

Veronica, Pamela and Frances

Introduction

I am the third child born to my parents Charles and Ruby Orsborn. I entered this world on 16 June 1937.

The road has not been an easy one. A lot happened in my childhood; quite a lot I wish that I could forget. I was brought up during the war years which was very unsettling. I was evacuated to two different billets and sent away to a home and a convent. I have very few good memories.

I have always been a rather solemn girl. When I was young I was very religious, always frightened to do something wrong in case I went to hell. It has taken me a lifetime to realise that I was afraid of my mother.

I was the odd one out in my family, taking life too seriously and never being able to relax. I felt a bit like Cinderella, having to do the housework, including piles of ironing, from a very young age. We had to light the kitchen range and boil our hot water on that.

Looking back, I realise I had a very disruptive childhood with many changes. Much of it might have seemed to be just 'normal' at the time, but today's generation would probably describe it as a childhood filled with loss and uncertainty.

The following are details of my immediate family:

Father Charles Anthony Spencer Orsborn, born 31 May 1902
Mother Violet Ruby, born 22 December 1911
Sister Josephine, born 5 May 1931
Sister Frances Rose, born 2 January 1936
Sister Pamela Winifred, born 9 October 1940
Sister Theresa, born 2 December 1946
Brother, stillborn 1948
Brother Anthony Charles Spencer, born 2 October 1950
Sister Margaret Louise, born 24 May 1952

Chapter One

During World War II, roughly 3.5 million children were evacuated from major cities in the UK to keep them safe. My first memory is when I was evacuated to Bournemouth with my sisters, Josephine and Frances. I must have been very young but I do remember that Josephine had a fall and hurt her elbow. The people in our billet were not very caring: they didn't even clean it or cover it up, and I have always thought that the fall had something to do with her illness as she died in 1948 from Hodgkin's disease. She was a lovely girl.

I also recall that the people who we stayed with used to make us take turns to pray with them every evening. The other two had to go to bed.

One day we were out for a walk and we heard planes overhead. They came quite low we could hear machine guns. We were very frightened. We ran along the road knocking on doors until someone took us in.

I can also remember planning to run away, but of course we didn't know how to go about it. We were very unhappy there, but I can't remember how long we had to stay. We returned home for a short while before being evacuated again. We had an Anderson air raid shelter in our garden and we often had to go into it. We had to have blackouts at the windows and we were not allowed to put lights on at night. Sometimes we would take shelter in the coal cupboard, which was under the stairs in the kitchen. We also used to sit under the kitchen table. We had gas masks, but I don't think we ever used them.

I have always believed that my mum used to work at night, but I have found out recently that she was dating American servicemen. I can't remember if my dad was there at these times or if anyone else used to look after us. My memory of this time is quite vague.

When I was about six years old, Josephine, Frances and I were sent to Aberfan, in Wales. We were separated into different billets (lodgings). Two spinster sisters looked after me and they were so kind and loving. Their names were Maggie and Enid, and I always called them aunt.

One of their nephews lived in the house with us; his name was Islwyn. We used to go to his family's home for tea on a Sunday afternoon, where we always had the cold meat that was left over from Sunday lunch. Islwyn and I used to play on top of the slag tips; including the one that collapsed on 21 October 1966 killing 116 poor children and 28 teachers. We attended the now infamous Pantglass Junior School.

I will never forget the day I heard about the Aberfan disaster. I went very cold when I heard it on the news. Later in life my second husband and I went to visit Aunt Maggie, (I had been back with my first husband some time before), and she took us to visit the graves. It was very emotional and we could never face going again. It was heart-breaking to see all those little crosses on the graves and to realise that most of them were children.

My time at 10 Wingfield Street, Aberfan, was very happy. Aunts Maggie and Enid looked after me very well. I used to go to the little shop nearby and buy sweets that were put in a little cornet-shaped bag. I can't remember having to use sweet coupons, but I must have, because that was the only way that you could buy sweets at the time. I felt very grown up being able to go on my own.

On Friday nights Aunt Maggie used to say "Let's have a look to see if you have any chickens in your hair." That meant nits or fleas. It was quite common during the war for children to have head lice.

Because I am a Roman Catholic, I used to go to my church on a Sunday morning which was just around the corner, and then to the chapel in the evening with my aunts and Islwyn. As I was growing up, I tried to make sure that I went to church. I thought I would go to hell if I missed mass. Although my sisters lived nearby in Aberfan, I seldom saw them. I don't know much about the billet where Josephine stayed. I remember that it was just around the corner.

Aunt Maggie   Aunt Enid

We never used to hear from our parents. There were no letters, and in those days not many people had telephones to keep in touch. Frances had a terrible billet. The people used to punch her and she had nits and fleas in her hair. Eventually my parents got to know about Frances' billet and they came and took us all away.

By this time it was getting towards the end of the war. Aunts Enid and Maggie wanted to adopt me but my parents wouldn't hear of it. I have often wished since that they had. I didn't want to leave Aberfan because I was so happy there. Aunt Enid died very young with cancer, but I kept in touch by letter with Aunt Maggie over the years.

My dad was in the Royal Marines and had been posted to a small seaside town called Towyn, in Wales, and so this is where we were taken. We lived in a big rented house. I didn't like it very much. There were rats and I was really scared of them. My mother used to work as a cleaner in the hotel opposite to where we lived. Sometimes we used to go down to the beach, which was not too far away. My dad never got posted to the front line. Mum used to say that she got him out of it, but I never understood how.

On VE Day there was a street parade and my mother dressed us up. Frances was Churchill and Pamela was his bride. I was dressed as a little black boy and when my mum took soot from the chimney and put it all over my face, I cried and I had white streaks down my face. I have always hated getting dirty and sometimes wonder if it is associated with that day. After the parade, my mum and dad went to the pub and took us with them. Everyone was so happy. I remember sitting on a soldier's lap outside the pub.

After the war we went back to our house in London. The train journey home seemed to take ages and I was very restless. I don't like sitting still for a long time, because I need to be doing something, and I can never sit still long enough to read a book. There were never any books in our house anyway and we were never encouraged to read. My mum would have thought we were lazy if we had sat down to read a book.

My dad had three brothers: Jim, Ted and George, and also one sister Helen, who we called Aunt Nell. They were all lovely but Uncle George was very special to me. He took my dad's place after his death. If I ever was upset, I would phone Uncle George and he always made me feel better.

Uncle Ted was a Japanese prisoner of war, and after his return, my sisters and I would sit on the stairs after we were supposed to be in bed, listening to him play the guitar and sing. The Japanese had treated him terribly. He had been starved, which affected him later in life. His wife's name was Elizabeth but we called her Aunt Vi. Our cousin Joyce is their daughter and we saw a lot of her when we were growing up. She lived with us for a while, and had a job as an usherette at the cinema.

Joyce   Uncle Ted

One day Frances, Joyce, and I decided to play truant from school. We went to Joyce's house and she climbed through a window and let us in, because she didn't have a key. We went home at the normal time, but what we didn't realise was that our mum had been to our school and asked the teacher if we could leave early to help her carry the shopping. We got such a telling off. I never played truant again; it taught me a lesson.

Uncle Jim had two children, Jimmy and Sylvia. His wife's name was Daisy and she died very young. She had tuberculosis (TB) and cancer. I can remember waiting outside the hospital for my parents when they went to visit. In those days children weren't allowed to visit anyone in hospital, not even their parents.

We never had much to do with my Aunt Nell. She had one daughter, Anne. I used to cycle over to see them sometimes. I don't think my aunt liked the way my parents were always in the pub, leaving us children at home. I am more in touch with Anne these days.

My Uncle George had two children, Barry and Carol. His wife, Aunt Win, wasn't very sociable. I can only remember her coming to our house once, and she was wearing a fur cape. I thought they must be well off!

Cousins Barry and Carol   Uncle George

At about this time Pamela was sent away to a hospital in Brentford, Middlesex. She had rheumatic fever and was away for several months. I have since learnt that she had TB as well. Again I can't remember anyone ever going to visit her. We didn't see her again until she came home from hospital.

Pamela was very highly strung and she used to play us older girls up a lot whenever we had to look after her. One day we were in the kitchen and she fell over her doll's pram and cut her forehead. I didn't know what to do, so I rushed out the front door and knocked on a couple of the neighbours' doors until someone came to help me. There was a Polish lady who lived two doors along and she came and had a look at it. When my dad came home he took Pamela to the doctors and she had to have stitches. She screamed the place down and the blood went all up the wall. I felt that it was my fault because I was looking after her. I don't know where my mum was, probably in the pub.

Chapter Two

In 1946, my mother was about to have another baby, and Pamela and I were put in a SSAFA (Soldiers Sailors and Air Force) home in Cirencester, Gloucestershire for a time. It was very strict there: our elbows would be banged hard if we rested them on the table when we were eating. We also had to do fire drill, which was sliding down outside the window on sheets that had been tied together. It was very scary and probably quite dangerous!

While we were there, we had a visit from the Duchess of Gloucester and I presented her with a bouquet. I was very nervous.

The Duchess of Gloucester at the back, me in the middle frowning,
Pamela behind the three boys in the front

A member of staff called Eileen took a shine to me. I went to visit her later on, travelling by train on my own to her home in Stroud, Gloucestershire. She lived in the country – there was no electricity or gas, and the toilets were outside. For light in the evening we had to use candles. It seems a million years away when I think of it now. We are so used to having toilets indoors. I lost touch with Eileen over the years.

When Pamela and I got back from the SSAFA home, there was an addition to our family, Theresa. I used to love looking after her and taking her out in her pram. It helped me later when I became a mother myself. I just adored babies.

In 1947, when I was ten, Frances and I were put in a convent, Nazareth House, in Bexhill-on-Sea, Sussex. Our cousin Joyce was also sent there and was there for about twelve years. It was a horrible place. The nuns were really cruel to all of us, and would hit us with the leg of a chair, which they always carried around with them. We were all given jobs to do and if you didn't do them properly you knew what would happen. My job was cleaning and polishing some stairs. They seemed to be secret stairs that I think must have led to the nun's quarters. These nuns had taken a vow not to speak to men.

We had to go to church every day but of course it was on the premises so we never actually left the building. We never had to leave the convent to go to school either, as that was in-house. Some days we used to have walks around the grounds all in a line. If we saw our cousin Joyce and spoke to her we would get into trouble. The punishment would be a good telling off or a slap with the chair leg.

The one thing that stands out from that time is the lumpy porridge for breakfast. If you didn't eat it you would get it for every meal until you did, and were given nothing else. Joyce worked in the kitchen and she sometimes used to manage to throw it away. She had to be careful or she would be punished. Because we were so hungry we used to eat our toothpaste called Gibbs Dentifrice, which came in a solid block.

Frances used to wet the bed and she got punished every day. I think her bed-wetting was probably due to nerves. We slept in a big dormitory and every morning we had to turn our beds down so that the nuns could inspect them. It was so impersonal and I never understood why we were there. We seemed to be pushed from pillar to post.

The only visitor that I remember was our Uncle George. He took us out to lunch. That was a special treat. I remember that I didn't want to go back to the convent after that. My uncle has always had a special place in my heart. He was not only lovely, he was funny as well.

That year Josephine became ill, and by 1948 we were back home. She had Hodgkin's disease, which is cancer of the glands. I can remember her standing at the kitchen table doing the washing, and saying to me, "Veronica, feel the lumps down my back." Even though she was so ill, she continued to work at home, and also had a job in a factory that made drugs. She went into a convalescent home in Margate, but it didn't do her any good.

Josephine   Josephine and a patient at Margate

My last memory of her was when she went into St James Hospital, Balham, London. I went on the bus with her but couldn't go all the way, as children weren't allowed in. Before I got off the bus she said to me, "Don't forget the cauliflower." She was a proper little mum and a really lovely girl.

A few days later my mum came into our bedroom and told me and my sisters that Josie had died. The date was 3 April 1948, just a month before her seventeenth birthday. We all sobbed our hearts out and couldn't believe that we would never see her again.

Her body lay in the coffin in our front room before the funeral, and my mother made us girls hold her hand and kiss her. It felt awful – she was so cold. My cousin Jimmy came to see her and he also broke down in floods of tears. He was very fond of Josie and was about the same age.

I still carry her rosary around with me even though it has fallen to pieces. It is in a little leather pouch and was given to her by the Bishop when she was so ill. She certainly deserved to go to heaven. I will never forget her and think about her a lot. Such a lovely girl shouldn't have died so young.

Soon after, my mother had a little boy who was stillborn. We were all very upset, especially my dad because it was his first son. Josephine had said to my mum just before she died, "I hope you have a little boy." I have always thought that the baby boy went to be with her.

I haven't got many memories of my grandfather on my dad's side, but I believe he died that same year. He had the same names as my dad but in a different order: Spencer Charles Anthony Orsborn. We were told that he was very good at tap dancing but I never saw him dance. He was a fruit and vegetable salesman and went around on a horse and cart delivering to houses. I can remember him in his coffin in the front room and us girls had to kiss him just like we did with my sister. I have never wanted to see a dead person since. I would rather remember them alive.

My dad told us that when he was very young, about twelve, he used to smoke and one day his dad said to him, "Have you been smoking Charlie?"

My dad replied, "No, Dad." Five minutes later he was doing handstands against the wall and all the cigarette ends fell out of his pocket!

Chapter Three

After the war when we were all back home, my mother began to take in lodgers. They were mostly men. This rented house was in Tooting, South London, and had four bedrooms, three reception rooms, a scullery and an outside toilet, which was in a wooden lean-to. We had a kitchen range and an open fire. There was no central heating and it was freezing when we got up in the morning. We didn't have any running hot water either. I didn't enjoy sharing our house with lodgers. I vowed that when I grew up I would never have any in my house.

One day my sister Frances and I got into an argument about something, and she picked up a poker that had been in the fire and whacked me across the leg with it. I screamed! She hadn't realised that it was still very hot even though the red glow had gone. I had the marks on my leg for a long time. She didn't only hit me once, but twice!

Veronica outside our house

There were rats in the toilet and in the back garden. We were always scared to use the toilet. There was no luxury of toilet paper either; we had to use newspaper. We used to keep chickens at the bottom of the garden and I think that is what encouraged the rats.

Sometimes we would have our own bedroom which seemed like heaven, but it was always short-lived. As soon as there was a chance of another lodger my mum would give them our room. If it meant more money she would cram them in. We would come home from school, or work when we got older, and find that we were sharing again. There were times when there would be four of us in the same bed including the young ones, and I would wake up in the night and find that I was very wet from where the youngest had wet the bed. It was horrible!

At times the dining room would be turned into a bedroom and more often than not the front room too. Often two men would share one bedroom, or a married couple.

An Irish couple lived with us at one point, and they used to have a wash and do the washing up in the same water. The wife of another couple got ill: she had TB and meningitis, and was admitted to hospital. The house then had to be fumigated.

An old French lady who lodged in the front room used to walk around her room in the nude. We would look through the window and have a laugh. We couldn't understand a word that she said. I don't know what she did for a living; she seemed to be in her room most of the time.

There was no privacy. The only place that you could have a wash was in the scullery. You never knew who was coming through the door as it was the only way to get to the toilet, and because there were so many people in the house it was inevitable that someone would come through. I used to get very embarrassed and hated getting undressed to have a wash.

It didn't seem to worry our mum; she used to come down in the morning in her bra with a jumper or blouse around her neck, ready to get dressed after she had a wash. As long as she was getting paid for having the lodgers she didn't care. My dad was a very quiet man and never seemed to say much. I don't think he knew half of what went on in our house.

Occasionally we used to go to Tooting Broadway to visit the slipper baths, also known as the bathhouse. There was a ladies' and men's section. There were several baths and if you wanted more hot or cold water, you had to shout out, "More hot in number three please." You weren't allowed to stay for long because the attendant would tell you to hurry up.

I hated how my mum used to carry on with some of the men. I caught her one morning being very intimate with an Irish lodger in his room, when I had to walk from my room through his to get to the rest of the house, as the two rooms were inter-connected. This man was well aware of my disapproval, and every time he looked at me, he would smirk.

Some days there wasn't much for dinner. My mum would always make sure that there was a meal for the lodgers on payday. She would be extra nice to them. It used to make me feel sick. If there was no tea or sugar in the house we had to go and ask the neighbours for some. I don't know if my mum ever paid them back. Sometimes she would make some toffee apples and we had to go out and sell them to people in the road. I hated doing it.

Occasionally my mum would send me to ask the priest for some money to buy shoes, otherwise we wouldn't be able to go to school. I found it very embarrassing. Sometimes we had to wear clogs. I wore clogs when I made my Confirmation at church.

One day one of the lodgers asked me to go and get something for him from the bedroom. The next I knew he was pushing me onto the bed and I had to fight him off. I was terrified. We had never been taught anything about sex but I knew that it wasn't right. Another time a different lodger pinned me against the wall. He said to me, "I will literally do you." I didn't really know what he meant, I was so naïve. I just knew it wasn't right.

There was a time when my mum looked after twins. They weren't very old. She used to put them in one of the rooms and not really bother about them. She hardly ever changed their nappies and they really smelled. It was awful. Mum was all sweetness and light and acted as if everything was all right when their mother would come to collect them. Again it was all about money.

We girls were always made to do the housework. Even when I was at work I had to clean the house from top to bottom before I could go out on a Saturday. My mum never said, "Thank you," she just took everything for granted. My sister Frances used to refuse to do it sometimes and she used to get a good hiding from my mum. I think I was just too scared of her and got on with it. But I must admit that I couldn't stand seeing the place dirty and untidy.

My mum and dad used to go to the pub a lot and sometimes when we were younger we would be left outside, usually looking after one of the young ones in a pram. Since I have grown up I have never liked pubs very much. I occasionally have a meal in a pub with my husband, but we never go just to sit and drink. I know that it is a way for people to socialise, but it doesn't appeal to me. I have never liked to see children in pubs.

Quite often when my mum and dad were out in the evening I would get down on my hands and knees and scrub the floors. I hated to see the place in a mess. My mum wasn't house-proud. She even used to leave the baby's dirty nappies in the lean-to (a windowless shed that was attached to the house) until she felt like washing them. I disliked living like that.

We never had any affection given to us by either of our parents. There was never a kiss or an arm put around us. Yet I was always very close to my dad. He was a very even-tempered man. I loved him dearly; we all did.

Chapter Four

My brother Anthony was born in 1950, and my dad was over the moon. We all were. We all spoilt him. It seemed very strange having a little boy in the house when it had always been girls. Unfortunately he had very bad eczema on his scalp. We used to have to try and loosen the scabs with olive oil.

He also had bad asthma attacks. This was something that was inherited from my dad's side of the family. He was a lovely little boy but always sick. When he got older he went to Lourdes to see if he could be healed but he was very ill when he came back and went straight into a hospital in Chelsea. I went to see him but was scared I would bump into my mum, who I hadn't seen for years, and didn't want to see then.

The doctors at the hospital told me that they thought Anthony's asthma was made worse by the fact that my mum and dad had split up. They asked me if there was any chance that they would get back together again. I said that I didn't think so. It was a sad state of affairs but there was nothing that I could do to alter the situation. It is always the children that suffer when marriages break down.

My dad was a baker's rounds man. The parish priest thought he was a milkman and that was his excuse for not going to mass on a Sunday. He had been a milkman in the past and didn't let the priest know that things had changed. He had a horse and a van, and worked very long hours starting at about six every morning. He would go and load up his van and then come home for breakfast. My mum used to keep me home from school a lot to do the housework. She used to hide me in the cupboard until my dad left after breakfast to make his deliveries. He wouldn't have allowed it had he known.

I thought it was fun to miss school at the time, but when I got older I always regretted the learning that I had missed. I vowed that if ever I had children I would make sure that they always went to school. Education is so important and learning is much easier when you are young. I have had to learn as I have gone along in life. I went to about nine different schools, which didn't help much.

From the age of about ten or eleven, my sister Frances and I used to take it in turns on a Saturday to help my dad on his round. We used to get some tips and we always knew which houses had generous customers, so we made sure that we delivered to them. Sometimes we would get sweets or fruit but we preferred money.

When we got home my mum would ask how much we had, and she would take half of it. Sometimes Frances would pretend she only got a certain amount and she kept more for herself. I was too frightened to do that in case my mum found out. We were all very good with money and mental arithmetic. My dad would tell us how much a customer owed that week and we had to add on what they had on the day. It was all done in our heads. There were no calculators in those days.

I can remember how much a large loaf of bread cost at that time: it was four pence halfpenny in old money. That is the equivalent of less than two pence in today's money. A small loaf was two pence three farthings. We had a couple of customers who would have a dozen loaves and that cost four shillings and sixpence.

We used to love going out with my dad. It was a very long day and sometimes we didn't get home until seven or eight in the evening. It was very cold in the winter. Sometimes my dad would take me for a cup of tea in a café. If they had a plain steamed pudding and syrup on the menu, he would treat me. I always hoped I would be able to have it as it was delicious.

Sometimes my dad would let us take the reins and drive the horse and van back to the yard. We had to be careful because there were tramlines in the road and you could get the wheels caught in them. We had one horse called Mick who didn't like the rain so we used to put a sack over his head. One day we weren't quick enough and he bolted. We had an awful job to catch him and calm him down. We all loved the horses and got attached to them. We would help to take the harnesses off when we got back to the yard and lead them into the stables.

I used to get embarrassed when we walked through the bakery because I felt that all the men were looking at me. Once in the office, I helped my dad count the day's takings. There were high desks with sloping tops in the office, just like you see on the old films. I used to like the attention that the office ladies gave me. I always thought that it would be nice to work in an office like that, but I knew that my lack of education would not allow that to happen.

For most of my life I have felt self-conscious about my lack of knowledge. We were never encouraged to read at home; about the only reading material to be found in our house was an occasional newspaper.

Picture: Stowey House open air school. Veronica in front of lady teacher

About this time I was sent to an 'open-air school', Stowey House, at Clapham Common, London. I was underweight and sickly and that was why I was referred there. Two meals were provided at the school, breakfast and lunch. All the classrooms were made of wood and there was no glass in the windows. We had to sit in our coats all day and it was a job to write because we were so cold. The exposure to fresh air was supposed to help children who were delicate and at risk of getting TB

Tuberculosis was a major killer in the UK in those days, and the search was on for effective drug treatment. Streptomycin was already being used, but it was thought that fresh air, rest, and a healthy diet, together with mild exercise, was key to prevention and also recovery.

We had to play netball and I hated having to wear shorts. I felt as if everyone was staring at me. I can remember being taught some gardening. After lunch we had to have a sleep on camp beds. One of the teachers would walk around checking to make sure that we were not lying on our left sides, as it was thought to be bad for your heart.

The school was five miles from home, and that was too far to walk, so I had to get there by bus or tram which made me sick, so I'm not sure if the health benefits at the school outweighed the issues I had in getting there and back!

Although I can only remember seeing her once, I remember that my grandmother on my mum's side had her hair plaited over her ears. I think they called the style 'earphones'. When she died the man who she had been living with in Surrey came to live with us. His name was Ted, but we called him Pop. He was a dirty old man.

He kept his flat in Surrey for a while and he would take one of us girls with him when he went to check that everything was all right. He tried being familiar with me when we were in the flat, but I just pushed him away. I stopped going with him after that, and I made some excuse about not being able to go. I don't know if my mum ever knew anything about what he tried to do. Frances told me that he did the same to her. I felt a bit sorry for him because our house was full of lodgers and there was no bed for him. He had to sleep in a chair in the corner of the kitchen and he hardly ever had a wash. I think he was about seventy.

Pop

I never knew who my real grandfather was. Mum never talked about him. It all seemed a bit of a mystery. It has been said since that Pop was our grandfather but I have my doubts. My mum had two brothers and a stepsister. Uncle Fred, who looked very much like my mum, was married to Aunt Rene and they had three children, Paul, Dennis and Diane. We used to see quite a lot of them because they lived nearby. One year they took me on holiday with them. I can't remember where we went, but we stayed in a caravan. They took me so

23

that I could look after the children in the evening when they went out. I quite enjoyed doing that.

The other brother was called Jack. I can't remember if he was married, but I remember where he lived, which was not far away. He died from TB. I don't think he was very old. I went to visit him once with my mum. Aunt Enid lived in Mitcham, Surrey, which, was only a few miles away. She had quite a large family: I can't remember how many, but I think they were all boys. We used to go and visit her sometimes but I don't remember her ever coming to our house.

We never knew our grandmother on my dad's side because she died when she was just thirty-two. We were always told that she died in childbirth but I have since found out that she had pulmonary tuberculosis and meningitis. Her name was Ada. My dad was only thirteen when she died.

My Uncle George told me that a very rich person left my great granddad some money, but he gave it all away. Apparently there was an article in one of the main newspapers about it. He wanted his family to make their own way in life. They all had a very hard life especially after losing their mother at such a young age. My dad was nine years older than my Uncle George and he practically brought him up. He went everywhere with him. My uncle thought the world of my dad.

We had five cinemas in Tooting, The Astoria, The Granada, The Hole in The Wall, The Majestic and The Classic. The Grenada was famous because it had an organ, and sometimes before a film started an organist would play. We didn't go to the cinema very often because we were always short of money. If it was a film that we were too young to see, we would pretend that we were older and hope that we remembered the year that we were supposed to be born if we were asked!

There was a person who lived up the road (I think his name was Mr Stevens) who was involved with the theatre. One evening we were invited to his house and Norman Wisdom was there. He sang 'So Tired'. I have always been a fan of Norman.

The party, Norman is not in the picture

Shopping was a lot different in those days. There were no supermarkets. You just went into a shop and asked for what you wanted, and someone would serve you over the counter.

There was a company called David Greigs Provision Merchants, that sold dairy products, bacon, ham and cheeses. The thing I remember most about that shop is that they used to sell the butter loose, using butter pats (two wooden spatulas). They were lovely shops and always spotlessly clean. Most people would have a list of what they needed and that was all they bought. There weren't lots of items around to tempt you to buy, and most people didn't have money for extras.

Chapter Five

1951 was a terrible year, because it was the year that my sister Theresa died. I was out on the round helping my dad and when we got home we were told that there had been a terrible accident. There were no mobile phones in those days, so my dad couldn't be contacted.

This is what happened: Theresa was in her cot in the main bedroom where my mum and dad slept. She wasn't very well. There was an open fire in the room and it is thought that she got out of her cot and reached up to the mantle shelf, where the fire caught her nightdress and drew it in. My sister, Frances, was downstairs with Frank, the lodger, and didn't hear her. The front door was open and as Theresa came down the stairs, the flames got worse. A neighbour, Mrs Joyce, was walking by and rushed in to help. She grabbed something to try to douse the flames.

My mum was in the pub at the time. There was an inquest and my mum was lucky not to be charged with neglect. Although I didn't know this until some years later, my mum blamed my sister Frances and called her a murderer.

I went to see Theresa in hospital and it was awful. I shall never forget her poor little face; it will be with me for the rest of my life. The accident happened the day before her fifth birthday, and she died ten days later of pneumonia. It was a happy release because she would have been so badly scarred. I had bought twin dolls for her birthday, and I was looking forward to seeing her little face when she took the wrapping off. I had started to think that I would like to be a nurse, but after seeing Theresa, I knew that I would be unable to do that job, as I would have become too emotionally involved.

From left, Frances, Theresa & Veronica

Soon after this, I started to get very bad headaches. I was very sick and had a terrible pain, usually over one eye. I saw the doctor and he diagnosed that I was suffering from migraines. Sometimes I had to have an injection to make me sleep, as the tablets made me sick.

During that year I rode on the back of a tandem to Brighton. It belonged to one of the lodgers. He was the one who my mum eventually left home with and they moved to Margate, in Kent.

Veronica at Brighton aged fourteen

A new year, a new baby. In 1952 my sister Margaret was born. She is the one who looks most like me, although I feel that I don't really know her, because she was not quite three when I left home, and the rest of my family moved to Kent. I am the only one who has never lived in Kent, and I feel I have always been the odd one out. Out of all us girls, Margaret had the most stable upbringing. I used to love looking after her and taking her out in her pram. Having experience with babies helped me in later life.

Frances and I used to go to the Wimbledon Palais Ballroom. Ken Mackintosh, Syd Lawrence and Ted Heath were some of the bands that played there. I met a boy called Eddie one evening and went out with him for several months. We always had to be home early. There was no staying out until midnight. My dad wouldn't allow us to stand on the doorstep saying good night to our boyfriends; he would shout out for us to come in.

Eddie was very fond of me and was always buying me things. I liked him but not enough to carry on the relationship. He joined the army and used to write to me. My mum used to steam open my letters. She took a dislike to him because he had a scar on his face, and she thought he was a bad boy. He took me to meet his parents and I got on well with them. In fact his mum was knitting a jumper for me, but I never got the finished item, because one foggy evening I told him that I didn't want to see him again. I felt really guilty. I did write to him after that, but I never got a reply. I wasn't really surprised because he had a very long walk home that night in the fog.

That year was the only year that I can remember having a holiday with the family. We went to Bognor Regis, Sussex, and stayed in a caravan. My mum and dad seemed to be quite happy at that time. I used to help look after Anthony and Margaret while my mum and dad went to the club in the evenings.

Munday's Holiday Camp, Bognor Regis, Sussex

From left: Pamela, Anthony and a friend   Mum & Dad

Later on that year I met Dave. He was in the Royal Navy and had been out in the Korean War. My mum and dad had met him in a pub when he was on leave, and they brought him home and introduced him to Frances and me. He was very quiet. He took Frances and me out to a dance one night, and on the way home the heel of my shoe broke so I had to hobble the rest of the way. We had a laugh about it.

He went out with Frances for a while, but then he started to take me out. He introduced me to his mum and stepfather. His mum was very fond of me and I got on with her very well. She was Welsh, and was in and out of hospital with cancer. We went to visit her in a London hospital; I think it was the Westminster, but I can't be sure.

This was the year that I officially left school; not that I was ever there very much. I was delighted to leave, but later in life realised how much I had missed out on.

I went to work in the laundry where Frances was working. We had to stand at a hot press all day pressing shirts, hankies etc. We got paid on a bonus system. I used to cycle to work, which was about five miles. I never wore any socks or stockings. I can always remember some older ladies saying to me, "You will suffer when you get older." How I wish that I had listened to them.

I can't remember how long I worked there, but eventually I left and got a job in another laundry. My mum knew how I hated working in a laundry, and with no qualifications there wasn't much else that I could do, so she suggested that I stay at home and run the house. It was something that I was good at.

I had previously applied for two jobs and was offered both. One was to train for a silver service waitress in DH Evans, Oxford Street, London. The other was to work as a live-in housekeeper, but my mum wouldn't let me do either of them. The reason was that the wages were not very good. By the time I had paid my fare to Oxford Street and home again, I wouldn't have had much left, and as my mum used to take half our wages, neither of us would have had much! The job as a housekeeper would have given her no money, as I wouldn't be living at home, and it would also mean that I wouldn't be around to do the housework for her. I decided that I would try staying home to run the family home. The plan was that my mum would get a job, I would look after the house and she would give me some spending money. This didn't happen. I hardly ever got any money.

I enjoyed looking after the house, but decided after a while to look for another job. I got a job at a local restaurant as a waitress. I had my own little room upstairs, and would operate a dumb waiter (a lift) to get my orders from the kitchen. I wore a black skirt and jumper or white blouse, and had a fancy white apron. I really felt the part.

I enjoyed the job, except for when some of the male customers wanted to get too friendly. One or two would ask me to sit on their knee. I had enough of that at home with the lodgers. I remember we did the catering at the Ascot races, and I had my seventeenth birthday there. It was quite exciting. I had to be up at the crack of dawn, and the manager from the restaurant picked me up at my house and dropped me off at the end of the day.

Chapter Six

My mum was never very good with money. She used to belong to a thrift club, a savings club run by someone in the pub. I decided to save ten shillings a week in this scheme, which was a lot of money in those days. I thought it would be nice to have about £26 at Christmas.

During the year my mum took out a loan to avoid a fine. She was supposed to pay it back, but never did. When Christmas came, there was nowhere near £26 in the kitty for me. I was very upset about it. She kept on saying that she would pay me back, but she never did.

That was my mum all over, always making promises, but never keeping them. There were times when she would promise to buy an item of clothing. I would be out helping my dad on his round, and all the way home I used to think, yes she has, no she hasn't. It was like a little game. I can never remember being pleasantly surprised that she kept her promise, but always let down. I vowed that if I ever had children, I would be sure to keep my promises.

We used to have a tally man come to the door (a form of credit where he would collect weekly amounts) and if my mum didn't have the money to pay him, we would have to go and tell him that she was out. I hated doing it knowing that she was in the house.

We had a girl come to live with us whose name was Pat, and Mum used to really make a fuss of her. I don't know where my mum met her, but it was probably in a pub. I can remember us girls resenting her. We felt that she was getting all the attention that we should have had.

In 1954, Frances got married to Morris, who was a sergeant in the army. They hadn't been going out for long. The wedding was on 26 June, at St. Boniface Church in Tooting, London. It was a very big wedding with eight bridesmaids and our brother Anthony was a page boy. I was the chief bridesmaid. The big wedding wasn't what my sister wanted, but she didn't have much say in it. My mum got into a lot of debt that day.

Frances had to help clear up the hall after her wedding. The day after, my mum sold her wedding dress. She and Morris came to live with us, and after a short time my sister had to sell her engagement ring to pay Mum for their keep. My mum tried to make her do the housework but her husband stopped that. Eventually they got married quarters and moved out.

Frances & Morris's Wedding 26 June 1954

Two years after their wedding a man called at Frances and Morris's flat to collect an eiderdown that my mum and dad had given to them as a wedding present. My mum had never paid for it, so the company wanted it back.

I saw a job advertised for assemblers and packers at a sweet and tobacco warehouse. I had no idea what the job entailed but I decided to apply for it and got offered the job which I enjoyed, though it was hard work. We had to assemble orders and then pack them in boxes. Some of the items were stacked on high shelves and we had to climb up to get them. I was always worried that the men could see up my skirt; women didn't wear trousers in those days.

Once we had packed the goods we had to price up the orders. This was something that I was quite good at and enjoyed doing. Then there were men who used to deliver the goods. A man called Bert was a lodger in our house, and also worked there, doing local deliveries from his cycle truck. He was a strange man and we girls used to tease him a bit.

I met my very good friend Maureen there, who I am still in touch with over fifty years later. After I had been there for a while, I was asked to help one of the senior staff in the shop. This meant handling large sums of money. I loved it and felt very honoured.

Dave used to call in the shop sometimes to say hello when he was on leave. He nearly always had a nice bunch of flowers to give to his mum. People used to say to me, "Anyone who is good to their mother will make a good husband."

One day when Dave was on leave, he came around to see me at home. I was in my curlers and making some cakes when he asked me if I would marry him. I was very surprised but excited and said yes straight away. We got engaged on Boxing Day and my mum arranged a little party. Dave's mum, stepfather Harry, brother Dennis, and wife Jeanne, came. I never used to like parties much. I didn't like all the fuss.

Our engagement party Boxing Day 1954

Because I was good with money and never liked to waste it, my mum got it into her head that I paid for my own engagement ring. That wasn't true. I did buy a signet ring for Dave and had it engraved with his initials. After we got engaged Dave bought a linen bale, which consisted of blankets, sheets etc. He kept it at his house and my mum objected to that. I used to buy little things and keep them for when we got married. In those days it was referred to as the bottom drawer. You added any presents that you had when you got engaged. I used to get quite excited when I looked in the drawer to see what we had.

Chapter Seven

At the beginning of 1955 I had settled into my new job and was enjoying it very much. But things were very bad at home. One evening my mum and dad came home from the pub and my mum started shouting at my dad. She used to drink Guinness and it made her very fiery. She was making a cup of tea and threw it at my dad, scalding his face. I was shaking all over. My poor dad, he didn't deserve that! I had begun to think about leaving home, and this incident made me more determined to do something about it. It was too upsetting to stay.

Dave and I had planned to get married later that year, in August. I would have only been eighteen but that didn't bother us. Dave was five years older than me and had travelled the world a bit with the navy. We got on really well together. However, things didn't work out as planned.

My mum had already bought my wedding dress without me even seeing it. I didn't want a big showy wedding, after seeing how my sister's big day had turned out, and knowing that it wasn't paid for. My mum wanted Dave to wear his naval uniform and he didn't want that either. We felt she just wanted to take over. In those days if you were under twenty-one you had to have your parents sign a consent form before you could get married and they had already done this.

One evening I had been out with Dave who knew how unhappy I was with the situation at home. My mum and dad were not sleeping together. Mum, two of my sisters and I were sleeping on the settee in the front room. The atmosphere between mum and my sisters and me was so bad, I just couldn't face sleeping with them.

Dave told me to sleep in my dad's bed. I was so naïve that I wouldn't have thought of it as being wrong. Later that night my mum turned up at Dave's house. She got him out of bed and woke everyone else in the house as well. She was ranting and raving shouting, "Where's my daughter?"

Dave replied, "She's at home."

He ran all the way to my house and shouted upstairs, "Are you there Vron?"

I answered, "Yes."

Dave waited for my mum to return and I heard him asking her questions. She didn't know how to answer him. That was the only time that I heard Dave have a go at anyone. He was a very placid person.

Things didn't improve. I never knew how the news got to my mum that I was planning to leave home, but it did. I arrived home from work one day to find all my lovely clothes had been pulled from the wardrobe and thrown around the room. This was the final straw. I treasured my nice clothes and was very fussy about them, and still am. If I saw something in a shop that I liked I would put a deposit on it and when I had enough money I would buy it. I never wanted to get into debt like my mum; I would sooner go without.

I managed to find a suitcase. I think I probably got it from Dave's house. I packed most of my clothes ready to move to my sister's flat. My sister had already told me that I could live with her and her husband, and I was looking forward to it.

I called to check with her if it was all right to move in, but found that she and Morris had gone away for a few days. My dad suggested that I ask a neighbour to look after my things until my sister came back home, and then he would bring them round on his horse and cart.

Once I left home I was much happier. It was like heaven. I had my own bedroom and the use of a bathroom, which was a real luxury for me. Dave used to come and visit me when he was on leave, and both my sister and her husband made him very welcome.

Chapter Eight

After I had been at my sister's flat for a few months, I developed flu symptoms so I went to see my doctor. I wasn't one to stay off work but he told me to go home to bed and that he would visit me in a few days. When he came, I asked him if I could go back to work. I will always remember his words. He said, "The work will be there long after you have gone my girl. Come and see me next week."

I went to his surgery the following week and he said I could go back to work. I don't know why, but I asked him if I could go for a mass x-ray; this was an x-ray of the chest, which was popular at the time. He agreed and I went to the local hospital and had it done. By this time I didn't feel very well and I was sweating a lot. I used to walk around with no shoes on and you could see my damp footprints on the floor. I didn't think anything of it and just got on with my job.

A few days later when I got home from work there was a letter waiting for me, asking me to return for another x-ray. I still didn't think much about it and went to work in the usual way, riding my bike. When I got there I told my boss that I had to go back to the hospital, and I cycled there in my lunch break.

When I got to the hospital I had another x-ray and I was asked to wait. The radiographer came over and asked me if there had been any chest problems in the family, and I said, "Oh yes, my mother had it."

"Had what?"

"TB." (Pulmonary Tuberculosis)

"That is what you have," she replied. "I want you to go straight to your doctor!"

I couldn't remember my mum ever being ill in hospital but she had told us she had TB and she had a little scar on her neck from having a phrenic crush, which was a procedure where the phrenic nerve was crushed to partially collapse the lung.

It was my eighteenth birthday, and I was so shocked at this news. It wasn't a very nice birthday present. After letting them know at work what was happening, I went to my doctor's surgery only to find that there was no surgery on a Thursday, so I went home and told my sister who was also very shocked. She was also a bit worried because she was two months pregnant, and TB was highly contagious.

I went to visit my doctor the next day and he gave me a letter and told me to go straight to the Brompton Hospital. I had never even heard of it, let alone knew where it was. By this time I thought that I should let my mum and dad know what was happening. I went to the house, which was in the same road as the doctor's surgery. It was the first time that I had been there since I left home. My mum decided that she would come with me.

When I got to the hospital I saw a specialist, Dr Livingston, who examined me. I had to go for another x-ray and some blood tests, then I had to go back in to see Dr Livingston who confirmed that I had TB in both lungs, and I was running a high temperature of 104. He told me that he was going to admit me for treatment immediately. I was stunned.

I was taken to the ward, which had about ten women in it. I sat on my bed and put earphones on to listen to the radio. I was oblivious to what was going on around me. Suddenly, the sister removed the headphones because the doctor was standing beside her and wanted to examine me. I was very shy and embarrassed about taking my clothes off.

Things were very different in those days. No one explained anything to me about what was going to happen or what treatment I was going to have. Because I was admitted from outpatients I didn't have anything suitable to wear in bed, or any toiletries.

I wanted to use the toilet and one of the patients let me borrow her dressing gown. While I was there, the sister asked the other patients where

I had gone. When they told her that I had gone to the toilet, she said, "That girl's not supposed to get out of bed."

The next thing I knew I was moved into a small ward so that sister could keep an eye on me. There were only three of us in the ward. It was quite cosy. I was on semi-absolute bed rest, which meant that I had to lay down all the time but I could raise myself up enough to have my meals. My bed was put on blocks so that my head was tilting back towards the floor. I was in that position for the next five months.

The first part of my treatment was having a streptomycin injection once a day and some INAH tablets. None of this meant anything to me the nurse just came and did the injection and gave me the tablets.

The day after my admission to hospital, Dave came to visit me. His eyes were red where he had been crying after he found out what had happened. He was home on leave for the weekend, and had gone to my sister's flat where he heard the news. His face lit up when he saw me. He had such a lovely smile and I was so pleased to see him. He bought me some clothes to wear and some toiletries. Later on his mum made me some pyjamas. She wasn't a well person herself so I was very grateful. She had cancer and had had a double mastectomy.

I found it very hard having to stay in bed all the time, not even being allowed to go to the toilet. The nurses used to give me a bed bath. The beds had to be kept very tidy and a visitor would never sit down on one. When the consultant or the matron came round everything had to be spick and span and we had to be very quiet. A lot of the time when I knew that the matron was going to do a round I would pretend to be asleep.

We were never told much about our illness. I knew that I had TB in both lungs. I had holes and infiltration. One evening I decided to crawl to the bottom of the bed to try to reach the drawer where my notes were kept. The lights were off but I had a torch. I managed to get my notes and started to read them under the bedclothes. I was scared stiff that a nurse was going to come in. I wanted to find out if I was going to have surgery. I didn't really find out a lot and managed to put my notes back without getting caught.

We had a few laughs in that ward. The two other patients were a lot older than me but I got on well with them. One of them would almost pass out when she had any blood taken from her, even if it was just a little pinprick. Sometimes we would have a midnight feast, but I can't remember where we got the goodies. The other two ladies used to have a Guinness, which was provided by the hospital as part of the treatment. It was thought to be good for you. I never had any because I found it too bitter.

After a while I was allowed to do one hour a day occupational therapy. I embroidered two tray cloths, which I still have. I have never been a needlewoman; I do what I have to.

The days in that ward were very long. We used to see old patients coming back in with no improvement, and I wondered if that would be me too.

I had to have a phrenic crush. Again nothing was explained to me. I was taken to the theatre and laid on a table. My face was covered up with something like a box with a cloth draped over it. The surgeon put some local anaesthetic in my neck. After a few minutes he made an incision and then cut the phrenic nerve. I can remember my legs shooting up in the air. Apparently that indicated that the job had been done. The surgeon was singing when he was operating. I was petrified. A few stitches were put in and I was taken back to the ward.

This procedure was discovered when a surgeon cut the nerve by mistake but found it helped his patient. After that, phrenic crushes became routine treatment to rest the lung, and it was what my mum had done too.

After a few months, Dr Oakley, (we used to call her Annie behind her back,) arrived at my bed with a couple of nurses and a trolley. I had no idea what was going to happen to me. She said, "We are going to give you a new treatment." This was called a pheno peritoneum, PP for short. A thick needle was inserted into my stomach and air pumped in to collapse the lung. It was done in an attempt to rest the lung so it could heal. Before it was done for the first time I was given a local anaesthetic. I had to have this procedure repeated weekly for the next two and a half years.

During my stay in the Brompton Hospital, apart from my mum visiting me once, I only had visits from Dave when he was on leave. His mum wanted to visit me but she was too ill. Hospitals were very strict in those days about visiting: you were only allowed one visitor at a time. Visiting times were Sunday and Wednesday from 2 until 3 pm.

I think the nature of my illness put people off visiting because it was such a contagious disease. Frances couldn't visit me because of her pregnancy.

After I had had about 160 injections they were stopped and I started a different treatment which was para-aminosalicylic acid (PAS). It was a big tablet like rice paper with powder inside. I had to take ten of those a day and I hated them. I preferred the injections.

After the change in my treatment I was told that I could start going to the toilet myself. It was heaven! I thought after being in bed for five months that I would be very shaky, but I was fine. The next thing I was allowed was to have my hair washed; that was bliss. They were getting me ready to go to a sanatorium in Frimley, Surrey.

The day came when I had to leave. It was very strange after being in that little ward for nearly six months. The ambulance was waiting and I said my goodbyes and left. It was quite an emotional time.

Chapter Nine

I had no idea what the sanatorium would be like, so I was surprised to find that it was such a large building, and the grounds seemed never-ending. I went back in my shell for a while until I got to know some of the patients and staff. The one thing that the Brompton Hospital had done for me was to bring me out of my shell a bit. I hardly used to say anything before going there. I really had lived a sheltered life.

Once I had been shown where my bed was, I had a routine check by the doctor, and began to settle in. There was a snooker table and table tennis, but I had never played any of those things, so I didn't bother. I don't really remember how I spent my time. I used to write to Dave every day and look forward to hearing from him. He would write as often as he could and visit me when he was home on leave.

Things at Frimley were very different from the hospital. We had to take our own temperature in the mornings and make our own beds. This didn't come as any hardship to me because I was very domesticated. We still had to rest during the day. All patients were assessed individually and I started by doing a certain walk a day, called 'once around the track'. This was increased gradually. Progress was closely monitored.

At Christmas, the staff, including the doctors, did their best to make it a special time. I have still got the lunch menu, which was signed by the staff. I knitted myself a nice red cardigan and I had a new skirt to wear. I wanted to look nice and warm for the festive season. Most of the patients were friendly. I got talking to a male patient and we used to have a chat now and again. One of the other patients told Dave when he came to visit me, that I had been fraternising with another patient. I couldn't believe it. I laughed when Dave told me, and assured him that there was nothing in it, just friendship.

Christmas at Frimley

Veronica to the left of the doctors

In February I received a letter from Dave and in it he wrote, "I need you more than ever now." He added that he would see me soon. I guessed that something must have happened to his mum and that he couldn't put it into words when writing to me.

One of the patients, who had her own room, let me use it the next time that Dave came to visit. He was wearing a black tie, and I didn't need to ask; I knew that his mum had died. We hugged each other. There was no need for words. He told me he had just got back to his ship when he got a message that his mum was very ill. He got compassionate leave and went straight back home. He sat up with his mum all night. He thought the world of his mum even though she had walked out on him, his dad and brother. She was only forty-eight, such a young age to die. I was also very fond of her. I can remember her saying to us when we were going out, "If you can't be good, be careful." I was too innocent in those days to know what she meant. She was never able to visit me at Frimley as she had planned to.

The next few months went by and there were various things going on. I took part in a play, 'Dial M for Murder'. I was very nervous but got through it without forgetting my lines. In the end I quite enjoyed it but once was enough.

Picture of play 'Dial M for Murder'

At one point I was allowed home for a weekend. Dave came and collected me and took me back to his house. It was very strange not having his mum there. He took me shopping and bought me a lovely coat, shoes and handbag to match. I can still picture them. The coat was a deep turquoise and the shoes and handbag were tan. We went out to the pictures one evening and we saw a Danny Kay film, 'Hans Christian Anderson'. We really enjoyed it and it was nice just being together, but all too soon I had to go back to Frimley.

Just after this, and before I was discharged from the sanatorium, Dave joined his ship and went out to the war in the Suez. He still used to write to me every day. Sometimes I would receive three or four letters at the same time.

I didn't know where I would live when I was discharged from the sanatorium. Originally I was going to stay at Dave's mum and stepfather's flat, but since his mum had died things had changed. Harry, Dave's stepfather, said that it would still be all right for me to stay, but I wasn't sure what people would say about a young girl staying under the same roof with a man in his sixties. However, I decided to take up his offer.

Things were being arranged for my discharge. I would be unable to go to work for a while and unable to do the job I was doing before I was ill. I would have to have a check-up at the Brompton Hospital every month. Arrangements were made for me to attend Kings College Hospital, Camberwell, London, for my PP treatment every week.

I had an interview with a lady almoner (like a social worker) and I told her that I would like to train to be a comptometer operator, as figures had always been my best subject. She said that she would arrange for me to go to a rehabilitation centre to do the training. A comptometer was a bit like an adding machine, widely used before computers appeared.

I managed to contact my dad once I knew my discharge date and he came to meet me off the bus and took me to Harry's place. It was lovely to see him after such a long time. It seemed strange leaving Frimley House, and in a way quite frightening. I was given a book of do's and don'ts and a green card, which meant that you were disabled. I tore them up! I just wanted to get on with my life. I didn't want any special treatment because of my illness.

In those days, benefit would run out if you were sick for a long time, and that's what happened to me. To get help you would have to go to National Assistance, which was frowned on. I had to work out how I would manage.

Harry told me that he didn't want me to do any cooking in the flat so I had to have my food out in cafés. I had saved a bit of money before I went into hospital which was supposed to be for my wedding. I didn't spend much of my sickness benefit while I was in hospital; only buying essential items like toiletries.

For the first few weeks I used my savings to live. I had to give Harry some money for my room. Then I decided to pluck up courage to see if I could get help. I went to the National Assistance Office (this was like Social Services these days). Someone took down my details and told me that I would be receiving a visit from one of the officers.

The day came and I was very nervous. I needn't have been. The man who came was very nice and understanding. He asked me a lot of questions, and I had nothing to hide. He asked, "What are you living on?"

"I'm using the little bit of savings that I had," I replied, and he told me,

"You silly girl, you can make a claim."

I responded that I felt very guilty about doing that, and his reply was, "You shouldn't, you're a genuine case and you're entitled to it."

I was pleased that I wasn't going to have to use all my savings.

I received a letter with an appointment to start at the Rehabilitation Centre. It was quite a long way from where I was living. I was very nervous on the first day. It was a bit like going back to school. In a sense it was, because you had to start with the basics.

I had to catch a bus at 7 am. That didn't worry me because I had always been an early riser. I felt very self-conscious sitting in a classroom. I felt that everyone was looking at me. I had always felt like that when I was at school as well. I was always too afraid to ask questions if I didn't understand anything.

When I went to see my specialist for my next check-up I asked when I could start work. He said that I could go part time which was a relief, as I didn't like not being at work.

Harry worked at a laundry as a van driver, and one day he came home and said, "They are looking for a pricing clerk at work, and I wondered if you would be interested?"

Of course I was. I rang Hayes Laundry and was given a date for an interview. I was very excited and also nervous. I didn't expect to get the job because I had never done any office work before.

The interview went very well and I was asked when I could start. I was surprised to be told that I had got the job, which was full time. I had mentioned my illness during the interview but I never said that I was only supposed to work part time. I explained that I was attending a rehabilitation centre and that I needed to inform them I was leaving to start work. I went to the centre the next day and told them I was starting a job the following Monday and they wished me well.

I arrived at the laundry on the Monday feeling very nervous and had to report to the boss's office for a little pep talk. Then I was taken to my section, which was a bit like being at school. There were two lines of desks with about eight ladies in total facing two other desks where the supervisor and her assistant worked. They handed out the work, which consisted of cards with items of clothing or household items, and prices were listed on sheets. We had to price the items that had been listed.

I soon got into the job and I was enjoying it. I found it very easy and didn't have to think about it too much. The staff were very friendly. We had our own canteen and had a fifteen-minute break in the morning and afternoon, and an hour for lunch. That was the time when I was able to get to know some of the other girls. I still remain friends with one person who worked in that office. I can't remember there being any men in the office except the management.

I would be very tired when I got home at night, and wondered if I had done the right thing going full time, but that was me – in for a penny in for a pound. I had something to write to Dave about now. He would be pleased for me but worried about me working full time.

After I had been there for two or three months, I was called to the boss's office. I wondered what I had done wrong, but I had a pleasant surprise: I was offered a position in the wages office. This meant more money. I started in the new office and the set up was the same as in the pricing section with two lines of desks. The only difference was that ladies working on adding machines occupied one line of desks. Those on the other side, which now included me, were working on the payroll.

Most of the work was done by hand and entered onto a large sheet. There was a small part that had to be put through a big machine – I can't remember what it was called. It seemed really antiquated even in those days. I had to work out the person's wages and deduct the tax and national insurance stamp and then it would go to the cashier, who would put the money in envelopes with the pay slip. I really enjoyed my job.

One day when I got home from work, Harry said that he had something to tell me, and asked, "What would you say if I said that I was going to get married again?"

Although I was a bit surprised, I said that it was nothing to do with me, and he must do as he wished. Eventually I was introduced to his lady friend. Her name was Chris. She had been widowed for eleven years and had a son, John, who was sixteen. I liked Chris very much and got on well with her. It was quite a while before I was introduced to John.

The wedding was planned for November, when Chris and John would be moving in. Although there was room for me to carry on living in the flat, I was asked to look for somewhere else. Chris didn't like the idea of her son being in the next bedroom to me. I don't know if it was John or me that she didn't trust!

I found a ground floor furnished flat in Brixton. It had a front bedroom, living room and scullery, (which was like a small kitchen). The toilet was outside in a little yard.

I was able to use the bedclothes that Dave had bought ready for when we got married. I earned £5 a week, and the rent was £3/10s a week. Dave started to send me money to help with the rent, pinned to his letters, which were censored; and none of it ever went missing. I wouldn't have had a lot of money for food and fares without his help.

An advantage of my new home was that it was a lot nearer to my job, so I saved a bit of money and time in travelling. I got to like my little flat and I could come and go as I pleased. I often wonder what I used to do with my time because there was no television and I can't even remember having a radio. It was a bit lonely and money was scarce. There was a very nice elderly couple who lived upstairs but I didn't see much of them. They kept themselves to themselves.

My sister and her husband had moved to Borden, in Hampshire, and I went to visit them one weekend. I can remember going to the local church. I used to be very religious and didn't like missing mass on a Sunday or a holy day.

November came and Chris and Harry got married. I didn't get an invite to the wedding and often wondered why! I had met John by this time; who was very shy. I found that I could talk to him easily and got on with him very well. Chris and Harry had bought a television and when I used to visit, John and I would look at the news about the Suez war. Not that there was much shown in those days, and Dave was not able to put much in his letters, so I was very much in the dark.

One of my friends at work helped me to put a poem together which I sent to the ship's radio request programme, asking them to play 'A Tender Trap' by Frank Sinatra. Dave was thrilled to bits when he heard it. I have still got a copy of the original poem. It is as follows:

> A tender trap is my intention
> And keeping you in life detention
> I'm hoping you will find it jolly
> And never feel that you are sorry
> And when you hear this by Sinatra
> You'll be happy ever after.
> If you've a girl in every port
> I'm glad that I'm the one you caught
> I hope this doesn't sound too silly
> From me to you
> Your loving filly.

In December I got news that Dave was hoping to get home at the beginning of January but there was no definite date yet. We planned to get married soon after he got home. It was a bit awkward because I had to get my parents to sign another consent form, but I didn't want my mum at my wedding, as I didn't feel that she had ever been much of a mother.

Chapter Ten

Just before Christmas 1956, I got news from Dave that he would be home on 9 January. I was so excited. I was allowed to meet the ship when it docked in Chatham.

Finally the day arrived. I was on the train when I was informed there had been a derailment and the passengers would be taken by bus for the rest of the journey. Eventually I arrived in Chatham about an hour and a half late. Dave had been very worried about me, but had managed to find out why I was delayed.

He took me onto the ship to show me his living quarters. I was very embarrassed about going down the steps. I had visions of the sailors looking up my dress. I had bought a nice turquoise dress with a cowl neckline, which matched the coat that Dave had bought me before he went to war. I felt like the cat's whiskers as I met Dave's mates, and I enjoyed the grand tour of the ship, though I was shocked at the lack of living space.

We went for some lunch, and then we headed back to my flat. Dave was keen to see it because it was where we would be starting our married life. It was lovely to have him home and to be able to have some time together. We did a bit of canoodling and that was a far as it went. In those days a good girl didn't go any further; she waited until she got married.

In the evening we went to a pub to celebrate Dave's homecoming. He then went home to Chris and Harry's, where he would stay until we got married. This was a very difficult time for Dave because he had left for the Suez just after his mum had died, and he was now going back to the same flat where his stepfather had a new wife and stepson. When he walked in he put his arms around Chris and they accepted each other straightaway.

Dave was now on leave and he used to come to my flat after I finished work. I cooked dinner for us. We discussed the plans for our wedding and decided on Saturday 9 February. Chris very kindly said that she would do the catering and that I could go from their flat because I wanted to get married in Tooting, so I needed to show I was resident in that area.

Dave and I plucked up courage to ask my mum and dad to sign a new consent form. When we got to the house, my mum said that she wanted to see where I was living. A date was made and my mum and dad arrived. They signed the form and my mum said, "You will let us know when you have decided on a date for the wedding won't you?"

I said, "Of course." That was a little white lie. I felt sorry for my dad but I didn't want my mum taking over my special day like she did my sister's.

My mother had bought a wedding dress for me without me being with her to choose it, but I didn't want to wear it. Dave and I decided to have wedding suits made to measure in the same fabric and colour, grey. I chose a pretty pink blouse and the same colour cardigan, just in case it was cold. I had black high-heeled sandals and a simple feather arrangement for my head. I didn't want a lot of fuss and had no bridesmaids, unlike my sister who had eight bridesmaids and a pageboy.

The day arrived and I was very excited but also nervous. We were going back to our flat in the evening and the next morning we were going for our honeymoon to Dave's Aunt Win and Uncle Charles, in Penarth, Wales.

The wedding car arrived at the flat. My Uncle George, who was a professional photographer was taking our photos. Harry was giving me away.

We arrived at the church and were just about to go in when my mother turned up with one of my sisters. She started shouting at me. I was very upset and almost in tears. I made my way back to the car when my uncle came over to me and told me to ignore her. In the end someone called the police and had her removed. Of course by then she had spoilt the start of my 'Special Day'. I found out later that it was the priest who let my mum know about our wedding.

Frances came to the wedding with Morris her husband, and Andre, their little boy. Most of the other guests were friends. The ceremony went off very well in the end.

After we had some photos taken we went back to Chris and Harry's flat. Chris had laid up a lovely spread for us and we were very grateful. My uncle went away to develop the photo proofs and brought them back later that evening. Morris belonged to the 'Magic Circle' and kept the guests happy with a few tricks.

At last the time had come for Dave and me to leave and start our new life together. This was the most wonderful moment in my life, happiness at last.

We walked to Tooting Broadway and, as a special treat, caught a taxi back to our flat. The following morning we travelled by train to Penarth to start our honeymoon. I was very nervous about meeting Dave's aunt and uncle, but I needn't have been; they were lovely to me.

Dave & Veronica Barnes 9 February 1957

Book Two

ADULTHOOD

THE BEST AND WORST DAYS OF MY LIFE

Dave and Veronica 1957

Introduction

From left, Morris, Dave, Veronica, Frances and Andre, Harry and Chris

Book 2 covers the years between 1957 and 1979 when I went from being married, to widowed, to married again.

Back from our honeymoon Dave and I started our life together as Mr and Mrs Barnes in our little furnished flat. Although it was sparse, it was like heaven to us, just to be on our own. We had a very simple life. There were certainly no luxuries in those days, but we just enjoyed and appreciated what we had. Apart from walking, the only way to get around was by bus or train. The shops didn't open all hours, so if you forgot something you had to wait until the following day, or if it was a Sunday, the Monday.

Chapter One

On our honeymoon, we were made very welcome at Aunt Win and Uncle Charles' home in Penarth, Wales. We didn't do anything very exciting. It was time to get to know each other and to be together. We had never spent much time in each other's company, what with Dave being in the Navy and me being in hospital for such a long time. Dave used to go to the pub in the evening with Uncle Charles. Women weren't allowed to go into pubs in Wales in those days, but I was quite happy to stay with Aunt Win, as I was never one for a lot of nightlife anyway.

We had a wonderful week and then returned to our flat in Brixton. Dave had to rejoin his ship and I went back to work. My friends were eager to look at our wedding photos, so as soon as I got them from Uncle George, I took them into work. I felt that my life was just beginning. Dave and I made our own decisions. We didn't have to answer to anyone. It was a lovely feeling. I used to sit at work and daydream some of the time. It was all a new experience to me. This was our home and I could do exactly as I liked.

Once we were home, I had to go for my weekly treatment at the hospital. I knew this was going to go on for a long time, so I just took it in my stride. I felt lucky that I was still alive. If it weren't for the fairly new treatment I was on, I knew it would be a different story. I felt excited about being a new housewife. I didn't need any lessons to clean or cook, as that is one thing that I gained from my upbringing. I wouldn't let Dave in my kitchen. Men never did much cooking in those days. Dave used to come home on his leave days. He used to enjoy reading and he belonged to a book club, where he received a book every month. I always wished that I could relax the way that he did.

We lived a very frugal life; there wasn't much money but we were happy. There were no fridges in those days. Well, that's not exactly true, there were a few about, but not many people had them; Chris and Harry had a gas one. I had to shop daily. We always had a healthy meal, nothing lavish, certainly no steak. I didn't even know what steak was, and I had certainly never eaten it. We didn't have much heating, just an oil heater in the living room. The rest of the flat was cold in the winter. We had to snuggle up to keep warm, but that wasn't a problem!

One day for a laugh I got dressed up in Dave's uniform, it was a bit big for me, but Dave said I looked good in it.

Veronica in Dave's
Navy uniform 1957

Our evenings were spent listening to the radio, or Dave would read a book. There used to be some really good plays on the radio and you could imagine you were there at the scene.

I was a bit lonely when Dave wasn't home. There was a tree outside our bedroom window, and if it was windy, it would cast a moving shadow on the window which I found a bit spooky.

I did all my washing by hand, with the exception of the sheets and pillowcases, which were done at the laundry where I worked, as I got a staff discount. Not many people had a washing machine at that time or even a spin drier.

One of Dave's Navy friends, a Scotsman named Jock, came to visit us and we all went out together. We had a good day, and it was nice for Dave to have a chat with him about their Navy life.

Veronica & Jock 1957   Dave 1957

Veronica 1957

In the April of 1957, Dave was posted overseas again. I can't remember all the places that he went to. I know one was Copenhagen and another Venice – he didn't think much of that place. At least this time it wasn't to a war zone. I think he had done his share of that, what with Korea and the Suez.

This was to be his last six months of service. He was due home in the October. He would then be on five years' reserve. I missed him a lot when he was away. I never saw any of my family. Frances had already moved away from London. I made friends at work but they had their own lives to lead. Sometimes I used to speak to the old folk who lived upstairs. They were lovely people. I have always been very fond of old people.

One day a lady at work told me about an unfurnished flat that was going to become available, and asked if Dave and I would be interested in it. I said we would. It was a rare thing in those days to get an unfurnished flat. This happened just before Dave came home, which was very convenient. We went to see the flat, which consisted of two rooms. In the living room there was a sink in the corner and room for a cooker. The toilet was on the landing and shared with other people.

There was what was called fixed price lighting, and that is all you got. You couldn't have any electrical appliances. I had a gas cooker and iron. We decided to take it. The rent was £1/10s a week. Of course we had to buy some furniture.

We bought a bed, wardrobes and a dressing table for the bedroom; a table, chairs and a sideboard for the living room. We also had to buy a cooker. We didn't have enough money to pay for it all, so we had to have hire purchase, which I hated. We just had lino on the floors. There were no fitted carpets in those days, at least not for working class people.

The flat was in a big old block. It was called Jubilee Buildings, a bit like the old Guinness Buildings in London. It was at St Georges Circus, London, near Elephant and Castle. When we moved into the flat, Dave put a curtain around the cooker and sink area. I used to pull the curtain when I had a wash. I was so shy, I didn't like Dave seeing me undressed.

By this time, Dave was out of the Navy. He didn't have any formal qualifications, but found a job working for British Relay Wireless. It was a company that connected pipe radio, transmitting through copper cable networks to terminals at homes, schools and factories. He used to go to different areas. At one time he worked for several weeks in Basingstoke, Hampshire. It meant that he earnt a bit more money, and that was useful as we never had much money to live on, even though I was working full time.

On Saturdays I used to clean the flat by using a broom, dustpan and brush, duster, polish and a bucket for the water to clean the floor. When I had finished that, I did any washing and then went out shopping.

I so enjoyed having my own front door, knowing that once I shut it no one else would come in apart from Dave. The only thing that I didn't like was sharing the toilet with other people, as it reminded me of living with the lodgers when I was growing up.

We settled down very well and were very happy with our life together. Dave was a very easy person to live with; he was so placid. We had a milkman deliver the milk daily and he would knock for his money on a Saturday. One day he said, "I have never known such a happy couple as you." I thought that was really nice.

We never did much in our spare time; we didn't have the money. We might go for a walk or visit Chris and Harry.

Chapter Two

In February 1958, I saw my specialist, Dr Livingstone, and he told me that I could stop my PP treatment. I still had to continue with my tablets. It was wonderful not having to have air pumped into my stomach every week, after enduring it for two and a half years.

A couple of months later I thought I might be pregnant, so I went to see a doctor. He wouldn't examine me unless I had another female with me, so a friend from work said that she would accompany me. The doctor examined me and told me that I couldn't possibly be pregnant, because he had turned my womb upside down. He said, "You girls think that when you miss a period, that you are preggie," (meaning pregnant).

I believed what he told me, but it wasn't true. I started to have morning sickness. The next time I went to the doctors, I saw a different doctor, who referred me to a hospital. The doctor there confirmed that I was pregnant. I will always remember that day; it was my twenty-first birthday.

There was a bus strike and we had to walk everywhere. I had gone out without my door key and I was sitting on the front step waiting for Dave to come home. He bought me a lovely bouquet of flowers and we went out to see a show in the evening.

The news was a bit of a shock because we hadn't planned to start a family yet, but once we got used to the idea, we were really looking forward to the baby coming. It was good to know that I could have a baby, because we had already decided to adopt if not.

We didn't mind if it was a girl or boy as long as it was healthy. I was not looking forward to telling Dr Livingstone on my next visit to the Brompton Hospital. He had advised me not to have any babies for some time. When I saw him he was all right about it, and told me to take it easy and rest, but that's not in my nature, and I carried on working full time.

I started to knit baby clothes and got quite excited. I bought things like soap, baby powder and cream, which I kept in a drawer. I thought it would help with the expense after the baby was born. We would be very short of money after the birth, because I would have to give up work. I paid the cheap stamp (national insurance) and that only covered for industrial injuries. Women never went back to work in those days. They stayed at home to look after the children.

When I was four and a half months into my pregnancy, I went for one of my check-ups and the nurse examining me thought that she could hear two hearts beating, so she measured me. I had been asked on my first appointments if there were any twins in the family, and I said that I thought my grandmother was a twin. It didn't seem to be important.

I had to go for an x-ray, which was a bit uncomfortable, as it meant lying on my tummy (there were no scans in those days). The result showed that I was expecting twins. I was told to go home and put my feet up and take things easy, but even then I still went to work, as we needed the money to pay off the HP on the furniture, as we wouldn't be able to afford the payments out of Dave's wages.

When I left the hospital that day, I was very excited. I had always thought it would be nice to have twins. I decided to try to find Dave. I knew the area that he would be working, but not the road. I eventually found him, and gave him the good news. He gave me a kiss and a big hug. His face was a picture; he had a lovely smile. He couldn't believe what he was hearing.

I made my way back to work and when I told my friends and colleagues, they were very surprised. Several said that I didn't look as if I was having one baby, let alone two.

One of my colleagues, Miss Lloyd, asked me if I would be interested in a ground floor flat in Clapham Common. I discussed it with Dave and we decided to go to have a look at it. The flat consisted of a large room at the front with a bay window, and a room next to it that was divided by wooden doors. There was a room at the back and a small scullery (a kitchen area). If anyone wanted to go out to the back garden, they had to walk through there. The toilet was outside. There was a small garden.

Miss Lloyd was the main tenant and she occupied the first and second floor. There was an elderly lady who lived on the top floor. The shops were only a few minutes away, so it was very convenient. We decided that we would like to live there, even though the rent was a bit more. We were quite excited about it. It would be nice to have our own toilet, even if it was outside. It was also a lot nearer to Chris and Harry.

In the meantime, I was getting a lot of pain, and Dave had to call the doctor in. It was the one who told me that I couldn't possibly be pregnant. He looked rather shocked, especially when I told him that I was expecting twins! He told me to rest and not to go to work. I stayed in bed and Dave managed to pop home at lunchtime the next day to see how I was. I was still not very good so he decided to call an ambulance (you could go to hospital in an ambulance in those days when you were having a baby).

When the ambulance men arrived, they covered my head with a blanket, so that the neighbours didn't stare at me. When we reached the hospital, I was taken to a labour ward in a wheelchair. On the way there we passed a matron and she looked at me and said, "You will be out tomorrow, my girl." I suppose she looked at my size and realised that I had some time to go before my babies were due.

The Lambeth Hospital used to be a workhouse, and it was awful. It had bars up at the windows and there were no pillowcases on the pillows. It was very bleak and I was very nervous. I was only thirty weeks into my pregnancy, and with twins it was rather early to be going into labour. I had doctors all around me, prodding about. I was given an injection to try to stop the labour. Husbands were not generally allowed in the labour ward, but as I had such a long labour, they let Dave stay with me. He would rub my back because it was very painful.

After thirty-six hours in labour, I was taken into the delivery room and twin one was born at 8.50 pm on 7 October, 1958. The second twin was born minutes after. She was a breech baby, and as she was being delivered I was rather upset at what I saw, as she was badly bruised.

The babies were so small. They were 3 lbs and 3 lbs 1 oz. They had to be rushed off and put in an incubator. I wasn't able to hold them at all. I realised later in life that I never had that initial bonding that one gets at birth.

We had to choose names for them because they were poorly and they had to be baptised. We chose Linda for twin one and Christine for twin two. It was funny, but when I was carrying them, I had never thought of having two babies of the same sex. In my head, it was always going to be Linda Christine and Michael David. They both ended up with just one Christian name. The next day, the doctor came and pulled the curtain around my bed, he told me that Christine had died. It was a terrible shock and I broke my heart.

When Dave came to see me, he tried to console me, but it wasn't easy. We had to think about Linda now. She appeared to be doing well. The same thing happened the following day. The doctor came and pulled the curtain around my bed. He told me that Linda had taken a turn for the worse. Her breathing was stopping and she was going blue. The doctors were doing their best to save her but as she was so tiny, it was touch and go. The curtain was left pulled around my bed because I was very distressed.

Later that day, Dave came to visit me and when he put his head around the curtain, his face showed all was well. He was beaming, and his lovely smile showed itself once again. He told me that Linda had pulled through. We were both overjoyed. We knew that Linda would have to stay in hospital for a few weeks but that was a small price to pay. She would have to be 5 1/2 lbs before she could come home.

Chris had already started to knit some smaller clothes for the babies; they were so tiny. She was so excited. She was like a mum to me, more than my mum had ever been. In between the birth of the babies, Dave had to move to our new flat on his own. He was now living at Clapham and had a bit further to travel to visit.

I had to stay in hospital for fifteen days. It was decided before the babies were born that it wouldn't be advisable for me to breast feed because of my TB. The doctor said that it would have been too much strain on me. I could express my milk and take it to the hospital for Linda.

When Christine died, she never had a proper funeral. She was buried with another person, which is what they did at the time. There was no birth or death certificate. It was as if she never existed. I still feel really sad about that.

The day came for me to go home. I had mixed feelings about it. I didn't like to leave Linda in hospital but I was looking forward to seeing the new flat. I used to go and visit her every day but it was a long time before I was able to hold her. I was only allowed to look at her through a glass window.

I was standing looking at her one day, when another mother appeared, who had ginger hair similar to Linda's. This lady said, "Do you think that they've got our babies mixed up?"

I replied, "No, she is so much like her dad. I have no doubt that she's mine." It gave me a bit of a fright, but I was certain that there had been no mix up.

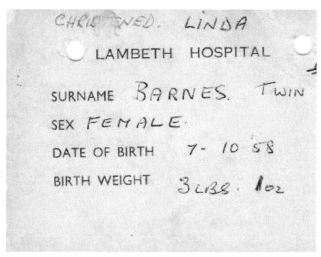

The tag that was on the incubator

One day, I was on a bus and saw a mother with twins. It really upset me, as I thought, "That should be me." I had to find a way to be sensible and grateful that we still had Linda. She was very tiny, but beautiful, and we loved her dearly.

Towards the end of October, I had my check-up appointment at the Brompton Hospital. When I saw Dr Livingstone, he looked rather surprised, because I shouldn't have had the babies until the middle of December. I explained to him what had happened. My check-up was fine and he was pleased that the birth had gone reasonably well.

Chapter Three

At last the day came when we could take Linda home. I was really looking forward to looking after her. Although she was so tiny, I wasn't a bit nervous, as I had all the experience of looking after small babies when I was growing up, although none was as tiny as Linda.

I soon got into a routine. Linda was a very good baby. She used to sleep a lot and she soon started to put on weight, even though I never woke her up to feed her. I can only remember having one really bad night, and that was when she had hiccups which wouldn't stop.

My friends and colleagues at work had bought me a baby bath on a stand and some other bits and pieces. I found them very useful. They didn't send me a congratulations card, because I had lost one baby, but sent a get-well card instead, to let me know that they were thinking about me.

Money was very tight. We had managed to pay off the HP, so we only had to pay the rent and buy our food. I used to make a shopping list, then total up to see if we could afford everything on it, and if not I would cross some items off. It was easier to know how much things cost in those days. Prices stayed the same for quite a long time, and when they did increase, it was only by a small amount.

There were not the commodities that are around now. Not many people had things like crisps or squash, as they were classed as luxuries. It wasn't that long after the end of the war, and things were very basic, but we didn't know any different so just got on with it. I think people were a lot healthier in those days. I have never been one for eating between meals.

I always did my own cooking; I made my own cakes (not out of a packet), and was well known for my Eccles cakes. Harry used to love them so I would always take some when we would visit. Dave didn't have a sweet tooth, but he did like my Eccles cakes, and he loved a fruitcake. He liked all the old fashioned cooking, like meat pies, stews, steamed puddings, and rice and macaroni puddings. People didn't make things like pizzas and curries. We just had good traditional food.

I still didn't have a washing machine, but washed everything by hand with the exception of the sheets and towels. Chris used to come over sometimes to look after Linda while I went to the launderette. I boiled the nappies in a galvanised bucket on the gas hob. I loved to see a line full of white nappies on the line. I had muslin to line the towelling ones. There were no disposable nappies in those days. I wouldn't have bought them even if there were, because I would have thought it a waste of money.

Once I had bathed Linda and dressed her in her lovely little clothes, I would put her in her pram outside the front of the house, to get some fresh air. There was never any fear of anything happening to your babies at that time. I would go indoors and get on with my chores, and every now and again I would go and check to see if Linda was all right. She was such a good baby.

Now and again we used to have a little get-togethers with our friends. Our living room was next to the bedroom, and Linda's cot was right next to the dividing door, but she used to sleep through all the music and other noises. I never believed in creeping around because she was asleep. We only had one little rug on the floor and we used to move it from room to room; mostly it would be in the bedroom but if we had visitors we moved it to the living room.

When we wanted to have a bath, we would put a tin bath on the floor in the kitchen. We had to boil the water on the stove, so we used the bucket that I used to boil the nappies. When we finished, we would manage between us to get it outside to empty it. There was a bathroom on the first floor where Miss Lloyd lived, but she never used it, as there was no running hot water.

Miss Lloyd had a tortoise that she used to keep in the coal cellar during the winter. When it ended hibernation, I would sometimes hear a clump, clump, as it would be walking through the house. I can't say that I was very keen on it.

We used to keep our dairy products in the cellar during the summer. I didn't like going down there very much, but didn't have a lot of choice, not having a fridge. I was always afraid there might be rats down there. The milk was delivered daily to the door. I think it was about four pence halfpenny a pint, just under five pence in today's money.

We went to Chris and Harry's for Christmas in 1958. Chris loved everything about Christmas and did everything to make it enjoyable. Although Linda was only just over two months old, it seemed to make things more special. Chris thought the world of her. She was like her grandmother.

Linda about three months

I was enjoying being a mother and cherished every minute with Linda. I was so proud to show her off to people. They could never believe how tiny she was when she was born. When Dave came home from work, he would make a fuss of her. She was so much like him to look at.

The summer of 1959 was really lovely. Linda was a healthy golden brown from where I had taken her out in her pram, or left her out at the front of the house. I had a sun canopy on the pram, but she still got the fresh air.

Linda 7 Months & Mum   Linda 7 Months & Dad   Linda 7 Months

One day I was visiting Chris and Harry when I bumped into my dad, whom I hadn't seen for a long time. He didn't invite me to go home, and I felt very sad because I loved my dad dearly. It was an awful way for him to see his granddaughter for the first time.

Dave had some time off work, so we decided to take Linda to see Aunt Win and Uncle Charles in Wales. We got a taxi to the railway station, and we were loaded up with all of Linda's things. I can remember we had a special little pillow, which had been embroidered, and we somehow lost it during the taxi ride. I was quite upset about it.

When we were on the train several people admired Linda, especially when they saw her drinking out of a cup. I had bought a cup that was shaped so that the drink didn't spill. When we arrived in Penarth, Aunt Win and Uncle Charles were so pleased to see us. They adored Linda. They had had two children, but had lost them when they were very young with pneumonia.

After that they adopted a little boy who was Aunt Win's half-brother. Her father had fathered the child out of wedlock. His name was George. He was grown up by this time and was away in the forces.

Linda outside Aunt Win's 1959

We took Linda down to the beach most days, which was a short walk through a park. We had a lovely break, and then went back home and settled down to our normal life.

I used to get up and do my chores, then take Linda out in her pram. We had the common nearby and you weren't afraid to go there in those days. I found my days were quite busy because there were no labour saving devices. There were no takeaway meals; I don't suppose we would have bought them if there were, because money was so tight.

During the year I had saved a bit of money (I think something like two shillings a week) to give Dave a surprise for his birthday in October. I bought tickets for the Black and White Minstrels show. It was the first time that we had left Linda. Miss Lloyd looked after her, but I worried all the time. We enjoyed the show, but couldn't wait to get back home to Linda. Needless to say, she was as good as gold.

I never wanted much out of life, just to have good health and to be happy. Life is what you make it really. I was glad that I didn't have to endure all the rows and being around the lodgers any longer. Dave and I never argued; he was such a placid person. I'm not saying that we never got annoyed with each other. I would just go very quiet and think about things. He never once raised his voice at me and he would protect me against anyone who swore around me.

One of Dave's friends from the Navy invited us to his home in Scotland for the New Year celebrations. I didn't go, because I didn't fancy roughing it with a young baby. They were going to travel in an old banger. There were no proper sleeping arrangements, so I thought I would be better staying at home with Linda.

I did miss Dave; he was away for a few days and I was looking forward to him coming home. I had no idea when that would be, because we didn't have telephones in those days, so I was forever looking out of the window to see if he was returning.

Aunt Win & Linda 1959   John's Mum & Linda 1959

I used to walk for miles with Linda in her pram. We weren't far from Battersea Park and I would go there when the Easter Parade was on; it was a lovely sight to see. One day I walked to Tooting to see Chris and Harry, and John walked with me on the way back. I caught something with my foot and John bent down and picked it up. It was a ten-shilling note. He never gave any of it to me; I thought he was a bit mean!

Chapter Four

One summer's day, Miss Lloyd took Linda out in her pram. She hadn't been gone long, when I suddenly realised I hadn't strapped her in. I was frantic. I raced down the high street and eventually found them. Miss Lloyd said, "I wondered why she was standing up!" I strapped her in safely and returned home, thankful that nothing terrible had happened.

In May 1960, I decided to go back to work so that we could save a bit of money and have some financial security. I hated the thought of leaving Linda. Women with children didn't go out to work in those days. I felt really guilty and dreaded telling Chris, as I knew that she wouldn't approve. There was a young mum opposite who offered to look after Linda. She had a little boy, David, who was about the same age. I was pretty sure that she would look after Linda well. She had a lovely home and was a very clean person.

I started looking for a job and saw an advert for a ledger clerk. I had never done anything like that before, but I managed to get an interview, and was asked lots of questions, then given a list of figures to add up. I was really nervous, even though I knew that I was good at maths. The person interviewing me, said, "I don't know why you were so nervous, you did really well." I got the job and started the following Monday.

My wages were £7/10s a week and I paid Sheila £2/10s for looking after Linda.

The company that I was going to work for was a wholesale grocery firm. The office was about two miles from where I lived and I walked there and back.

On my first day I was greeted by two Irish sisters who worked in the office, Helen and Maureen. Helen was married but separated from her husband; she wouldn't divorce him because she was a Catholic. Both she and Maureen lived with their mother in Paddington.

The manager, Mr Austin, was in an office nearby. I got on really well with him. He was a great fan of Shirley Bassey, and I used to pull his leg about it.

I soon settled in and learnt the ropes. I enjoyed the job because it involved a lot of figure work, although I had to deal with some fractions, which I muddled through, because I had never done fractions at school. It was great to receive my first wage packet. I decided that I would save as much as I could, putting it in my Post Office account one week and Dave's the next.

Sometimes there were dented tins of fruit that were offered to us at half price. The senior manager, whose name I can't remember, used to give me some cut ham now and again. He seemed to favour me because I had a husband and child.

Linda settled in very well with Sheila and her little boy, David. She enjoyed playing with him. I hated leaving her though. After I had collected her one day and we had got home, she patted her head and said, "This is wooden." She then pinched her face and said, "This is plastic." I will never forget that, it was lovely; so innocent.

I used to go to Colliers Wood to visit my friend, Maureen. She used to live in a flat at her mother and father's house, and they later moved into a council maisonette which was very nice. Maureen's little girl, Maria, was born five months before Linda. Maureen would cook a meal for us, and then I would get the bus back home. Other times she would come and visit me. It was nice to catch up on all the news, as in those days we didn't have a telephone.

Linda & Maria August 1960

Linda December 1960

One day Dave decided to take Linda to see his family in Christchurch, Hampshire (now Dorset). He wanted to try and find out where his dad lived. He hadn't seen him since he was fourteen, when his parents' marriage broke up and he went into the Navy. He was now coming up to twenty-eight. He wanted me to go with him but I couldn't take time off work when I hadn't been there very long. He was a bit upset about it.

He firstly went to see his brother, Dennis, and his wife Jeanne, and family. At that time, they had two little boys, David and Stephen. They fell in love with Linda. Dennis was able to tell Dave where his dad and a lady called Elsie were living, and they made him and Linda very welcome. They lived in a tied house (one that was owned by his employer). He rang up from his dad's house and spoke to me on the phone at Sheila's house.

I was so pleased that he had got back with his family again, especially because he had lost his mum. A while later, Dave took me to see his dad for a weekend, and I was surprised to see how alike they were. His family fell in love with Linda and made a fuss of her.

We went to see Dennis and Jeanne again. I had already met them when we got engaged but they never came to our wedding, because although they were invited they wouldn't come because I was a Catholic. People used to be very funny about going into churches that weren't their denomination. After seeing Linda, Dennis and Jeanne decided to have another baby. They had a little girl and called her Frances. Dennis was besotted with her, she couldn't do anything wrong, but I don't think she was an easy child. They gave her everything and she was very spoilt.

Granddad Barnes, Veronica & Linda Sep 1961 (Judy the dog)

Elsie, Granddad Barnes & Linda Sep 1961

Chapter Five

In 1961, Dave decided to apply to join the Fire Brigade, who were keen to have ex-servicemen. He had filled in the forms once before, and made a mess of them, but now he had to act quickly because he was nearly twenty-nine and the age deadline was thirty. He got an interview and was accepted for training. There was no guarantee that he would pass, not all candidates did, but he was one of the lucky ones. He had to do weeks of training and it was really hard work. He had such a lot to learn about different chemicals, and that involved a great deal of reading. He was stationed at Lambeth and used to cycle the few miles to work. I was very nervous about him being a fireman, as it was such a dangerous job.

He had some money due to him from his pension fund when he left British Relay Wireless, so he bought a spin drier and a boiler. I didn't want a washing machine, but I liked to boil my whites, and the spin drier came in useful.

Once Dave finished his training, he worked long hours, different shifts, fifty-six hours a week. He did one shift that was twenty-three hours long. I hated it when he was away that long, which was usually at weekends.

This year we decided that we would like another baby. Linda was nearly three and we didn't want her to be an only child. I always thought that I would like to have four children. My friends Maureen and Arthur had just had another baby, John, and that made me keen to have another.

Some other friends, Maureen and Mac, came to see us; they lived just outside Brixton and later moved to Banbury in Oxfordshire. They were expecting their first baby. We all went for a picnic and they made a fuss of Linda.

From left, Maureen Mac, Linda & Veronica May 1961

John had a very serious motorbike accident in March of that year. He nearly lost his leg. The police went to the house to give Chris the news, and she was in a terrible state as it was something that she had always dreaded. The shock affected her hearing. John was in hospital for a long time and had a plate put in his leg.

It was a very hot summer. I found out I was pregnant and started getting morning sickness. Dave said to me, "This will be the last baby, I can't see you suffering like this again." Because Dave hadn't been in his job for long, he couldn't take a holiday, so Chris and I decided to go to Bognor Regis, Sussex, with Linda, and we had a lovely week. We stayed in a caravan and Dave came for the weekend. We took it easy and had most of our meals out. It was very hot and I got sunburn after sitting on the beach all day. I remember the day that we went home the temperature was 90 degrees.

Linda on the beach at Bognor July 1961

Later that year we found out that we were going to be evicted. I went to the Council to find out if we had any chance of getting a flat. We were put on the waiting list, but were told that there was no guarantee that we would be re-housed. It was a very worrying time, especially as I was pregnant.

When I was about five months into my pregnancy, I decided to give my notice in. The boss tried to talk me into staying but I told him that I didn't want to take any chances this time, not after going into labour ten weeks early when I had the twins. I worked my notice and left. Everyone was sorry to see me go and they gave me a good send off. I promised them that I would take the baby to see them after it was born.

I missed work and the money, but it was nice to be at home with Linda again. I never liked leaving her, but at least we had a bit of money behind us now and felt a bit more secure. I was also able to buy her some nice clothes.

At that house, when the dustmen came they had to walk through the house to get the bin. One day the dustman came and was staring at me. I felt a bit embarrassed until he said, "I know you! I went to the same school as you."

85

I wouldn't have known him if he hadn't said anything, and I was surprised anyone remembered me, considering that I was hardly ever at school.

I went to the Council to see how long we would have to wait to be re-housed. There was no way that we would be able to afford to buy a property. Even if we had the deposit, we wouldn't have been able to get a mortgage on Dave's wages.

When Dave joined the fire brigade we had to open a bank account. His wages were paid in monthly. It was hard at first because we had to wait a month before we got any money, rather than getting paid weekly.

I had always been used to putting a certain amount away to pay the bills because I never wanted to end up like my mum, who was so hopeless with money. I always thought that she could have been comfortably off if she managed her money properly.

In February 1962 we received a letter from the Council, offering us a prefab in Southfields. A major building programme of prefabricated buildings had been instigated after the war to address the housing shortage. They were well designed and popular, dubbed 'palaces for the people'.

I had never heard of Southfields, but I found out it was not very far from the Wimbledon tennis courts. We were given a date to view it, which was a Monday. It was three weeks before our baby was due. We were very excited, and when the day came and after I had been to my antenatal clinic for my check up, (one of the nurses said, "We'll see you next week, if you don't do anything silly,") we made our way to the prefab.

There were four prefabs on the site and we couldn't wait to look inside. It was lovely. There were two bedrooms, a lounge, a kitchen with fitted cupboards and a table that folded up against the wall. There was also a fitted fridge, which we'd never had before. The icing on the cake was a bathroom and a separate toilet. The hallway was a nice size and there was plenty of room for the pram.

The rooms needed a bit of decorating. We met the neighbours who lived next door, and they were very friendly. It would be lovely to have our own front door and a bit of garden because Dave enjoyed gardening.

We knew that the move to the prefab was temporary because they were going to pull them down, but we would be offered something else when the time came. Before we left there, I asked Dave if we could go and order a bed for Linda because she was still sleeping in her cot, and we would need it for the baby.

We stopped off at Clapham Junction on the way home and ordered one. By the time we got home I was very tired and had a terrible backache. I asked Dave if we could go over to tell Chris our good news. He said, "You are not going anywhere, I'll go on my bike." He made me rest.

When he got back we had a drink and went to bed. I woke up at four in the morning and wanted to go to the toilet. Miss Lloyd had said that I could use her toilet at night, to save me going outside. She also said that she would keep an eye on Linda when I went to hospital.

I started to get bad pains and realised that the baby was coming. I went back downstairs and told Dave that he needed to get the ambulance. We called Miss Lloyd and then woke Linda. We told her that we were going to get her new baby sister or brother. She said, "Good, I can go to Auntie Chris's." Chris had offered to have her while I was in hospital and she loved being with her.

The ambulance came and I arrived at the little nursing home in Clapham called Annie McCall's at about 5 am. Before Dave left me he said, "Be good." I don't know what he thought I was going to get up to! There wasn't much time to prepare me for the birth. Our son was born at 5.50 am. The nurse had tried to give me gas and air but I pushed her hand away. After the birth, she asked me why I wouldn't have it. I told her that I couldn't stand having anything over my face.

We had decided to call our baby Trevor David. It had a nice ring to it and also sounded very Welsh. Dave's mother was Welsh – how she would have loved to have seen her grandchildren.

Dave rang up and the nurse let me speak to him. I told him that we had got a son and that he weighed 7 lbs 13 oz. He said, "Thank you sweetheart." I tried to get out of bed and the nurse told me to get back in. I was moved from the delivery room to a ward.

Later in the morning, Dave called in to see us. His face said it all, he was so proud. After the experience I had when the twins were born, it was lovely to be able to have the baby near me. Dave was on a night shift and when he got to work that evening and said that I had given birth, his senior officer said, "What are you doing here? Why aren't you visiting your wife?"

He was allowed to have some time off, so he cycled to the hospital. When he got there, he wasn't allowed in because he had seen me in the morning. I didn't find out about it until the next morning and I was furious. Dave should have insisted on seeing me, but he wouldn't make a fuss. Two days after the birth, John came to visit me. He didn't have any trouble getting in even though it wasn't visiting time. He would get around anyone with his charm. It was good of him to visit me.

Once again, Dave was left to do the moving on his own. He got the keys to the prefab and decided to do a bit of decorating before moving in. Chris was still looking after Linda and I knew that she would have been enjoying herself. There was no form of heating in the prefab apart from an electric fire and our oil heater. Dave decided to put electric wall heaters in the bedrooms and the bathroom, so I could keep warm when I had to feed the baby.

After I had been in hospital for a week, I was told that I could go home the next day. I was so excited after being in hospital so long with Linda. Dave had already brought my clothes in, so the next day I was all ready to go home. When the doctor came to the ward, the nurse pulled the curtains around my bed. The doctor said, "I'm sorry but we won't be able to let you go home today because your baby has got an infection in his water, nose and throat. He's also lost weight."

I was devastated. He then told me that we would have to be isolated. When we arrived in the isolation room we found it was very cold. There was snow on the ground outside and it didn't feel much warmer inside. One night

I took our baby into bed with me to warm him up. I fell asleep and when I woke up I was still cuddling him. I thought, "Oh my goodness I could have smothered him."

When Dave came expecting to take us home, he was shocked to hear the news. The nurse used to inject the baby with a big needle, and I would get very upset.

At last, after being in hospital for three weeks, I was going to be able to go home with our baby, Trevor. I was really looking forward to seeing Linda. Children weren't allowed to visit at that time. It was a long time without seeing her, but I knew that Chris was looking after her well. Dave collected us and we went back to our new home. As the saying goes, "A new home, a new baby."

Dave had made the prefab a home. The decorating looked good and he had put the beds up and arranged the rest of the furniture. The following day Dave went to collect Linda. I stayed at home with Trevor and waited for their return.

We all settled into our new home very well. It seemed too good to be true. It was lovely having our own front door and bathroom, also the luxury of having a fridge even if it was small. Linda seemed to be pleased to have a baby brother but one day when I was bathing him, she took hold of his hand and bit it. I was shocked but realised that she was jealous.

She had been the only one for nearly three and a half years and now she had to share our love. That was the only time that it happened. I told her it was naughty and after that I tried to get her involved when I was bathing Trevor. Dave and I had to make sure that we made a fuss of her. She adored Trevor really.

It was lovely living in the prefab. We had our own garden, which pleased Dave; he loved to do work out there. I can remember we had some gooseberries, which I had never tasted before. The neighbours were very friendly. Doll and Nell kept house for one of their sisters and her two daughters. The sister used to drive one of the MOD cars. They all loved Linda and Trevor. They were like family; always willing to help.

After I had been out of hospital for a couple of weeks, I had to take Trevor to the doctors because he had another infection. The doctor said that if it didn't clear up, he would have to go into hospital. Luckily it didn't come to that, and he got better. He was diagnosed with asthma and eczema, something that I had always dreaded, because my brother, Anthony, suffered with these conditions, and it ran in the family on my dad's side, mainly in the boys.

Chapter Six

I was feeling a bit fed up because I hadn't got back to my normal weight after the birth and couldn't get into my clothes, so Dave took me out and bought me a new dress. I thought that I would never get back to the size I was before, but I tried and eventually succeeded.

We decided to arrange for Trevor to be baptised and for Linda to be blessed at the same time. The date was set for 10 June 1962. We asked John if he would be godfather and Maureen, from where I used to work, to be godmother. John didn't think he would be allowed to do it because he wasn't a Catholic, but I checked and it was all right, because one godparent, Maureen, was Catholic. It was a lovely little church and not far from the prefab. Chris helped me with the catering and everything went off well. It was a nice day but a bit windy.

Maureen with Trevor and Linda 10 June 1962

A few weeks later my dad and my cousin, Jimmy, turned up at our door. I don't know how they found out where we lived. My dad told me that he and my mum had split up and that he was getting a divorce. The divorce was on 2 July. I felt really guilty because I couldn't go with him on the day he went to court. I felt so sorry for him.

My mum had moved to Kent with one of the lodgers. She then met another man, Frank Saunders, and eventually she married him. My dad never got over my mum leaving him. He still had the house in Tooting and asked Dave and me if we would move in with him. I said no, because I told him that I would always be living in fear of my mum turning up on the doorstep and causing trouble. My life was a lot simpler now, and I wanted to keep it that way.

My dad had bought a little moped bike; he called it Tina, and he started to visit us once a week. I used to cook him a meal and do his washing. He would take the previous week's washing with him when he went home. He was still riding his bike with L-plates on; I don't think he ever got a full licence. He loved to see the children and always gave me a pound to buy them some fruit. If the ice cream man came around, he would buy them an ice cream, and they loved that.

Granddad Charles & Linda June 1962

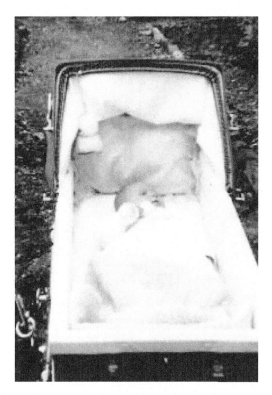

Trevor April 1962

Linda, Trevor & Paula (a neighbour)

Veronica Orsborn

Trevor's first ice cream Sep 1962

Chapter Seven

A few months after we moved into the prefab, we were invited by the Council to view a brand new flat. It had two bedrooms and under-floor heating.

The day came and we went to view it. It was in a high-rise building, which had become popular in the sixties. Everything was lovely and new and I should have been very excited, but I wasn't. I couldn't think where the children would be able to play. The shops were a long way away from the flat and I couldn't imagine how I would get there with two young children. Dave and I discussed it and I told him that I didn't want to live there. We went to the Council office and told them that we didn't want to take it.

The tenants in the other prefabs all accepted. I think they were too scared to turn the offer down in case they didn't get offered anything else. We were the last ones in and going to be the last ones out. We were a bit cheeky really, but I knew that if we moved there we wouldn't be happy.

Life went on for the next few weeks and then we got another offer. By this time all the other prefabs were empty. Eventually the Council were going to pull them down. I thought it was a shame and that it would have been far better to have refurbished them.

The next flat that we viewed was in Wandsworth. It was very small and had no coal fire, and no garden. It was a very old building in a very busy and noisy area. We thought that we might take it temporarily while I tried to find someone to look after the children so that I could go back to work and save some money to buy our own place, but eventually decided to turn that down too.

Back to the Council we went. When we told the man that we didn't want to live there, he never made any comment. We didn't know how many times that we would be able to turn down an offer, but it just didn't feel right.

A few weeks later we viewed another flat, this time in Brixton, which was not a nice area. When we arrived, we got the feeling that we weren't going to like it. It was so small: the second bedroom wasn't big enough for two beds. There was nowhere for the children to play.

Once again we went back to the Council and said that we didn't want to accept it. Dave was a bit worried that if we turned this one down, that we wouldn't be offered anything else, so he left it to me to do the talking.

We settled back into our normal routine and kept watching for the postman. Eventually a fourth offer came. It was in Clapham Common, a two-bedroom ground floor flat. When we arrived to view it, we thought it looked a lot more promising than any of the others we had seen. We opened the door and there was a separate toilet and bathroom just inside. The next room was the kitchen; it had fitted cupboards all around. There were two good sized bedrooms and a large lounge diner.

We felt so excited. Dave lifted me up and danced around the room with me. It was everything that we could have wished for. It had an open fire and a bit of garden. All the flats had a bit of garden, and they were all gated off. There was also a communal area, and a little storage cupboard in the porch where you could keep a bike or anything else that you wanted to.

We couldn't wait to go back to the Council and tell them that we would like to accept. I'm sure they were glad to get rid of us. Although we were excited about the move, we were sorry to be leaving the prefab. We would also miss our neighbours as they had become good friends.

I wasn't going to get out of the move this time. Moving twice in eight months was rather a lot, but the flat was worth it, and I couldn't wait. We arranged to move the next week. When the day came we went to say goodbye to Nell and Doll. We were rather sad; it felt as if we had known them for years, not just a few months.

We arrived at the flat and began to arrange our furniture and unpack the boxes. Dave had a few days off work, which was a great help. I went out to buy some new curtains for the lounge because it was a bigger window than any at the prefab. Although it had been nice to live in Southfields, it was good to be back in Clapham Common. We all settled in very well and Dave enjoyed sorting the garden out.

We got to meet some of the neighbours and there was one man, Mr Hicks, who was very friendly and lived on the top floor. The two top flats were larger, with three bedrooms. He used to have Trevor round sometimes and they would play with his toy cars.

Dave managed to get transferred to the local fire station, which was just five minutes away. It saved a lot of travelling time and was much better during the winter, which was very bad that year. It snowed on Boxing Day and the snow stayed around until April. The pavements were solid ice, also parts of the roads and gutters. I couldn't push the pram out and had to arrange for someone to keep an eye on the children while I went shopping.

One day Linda and Trevor were playing in the living room, when Linda pushed Trevor and he fell and hit his eye on the table. It swelled up and by the morning it was all black and blue. Dave had been on night duty and I was on my way to the doctor's surgery when we met him going home. When he saw us, he said, "What is the other guy like?" I told him where I was going; he laughed and said that he would take him. The doctor checked him, and said that he was all right.

That summer we decided to have a holiday at a holiday camp for a week, so that I could have a rest from cooking. I didn't fancy a big camp, like Butlins, so we found a smaller camp on the Isle of Wight. I remember it cost £27 for the four of us for a week. Our friends, Maureen and Mac who had a little girl, Debra, came too.

This year my dad went to Germany for a holiday with my sister Frances and her husband, Morris who was stationed there with the armed forces. He was a bit nervous about flying, because he had never done it before. He had a great time. He promised to take Trevor on a plane when he got older.

Dad getting off the aeroplane in Germany May 1963

Linda started school in September that year. I managed to get her into the local Catholic School, St Mary's. On the first morning she was very excited and trotted off quite happily. I was feeling rather apprehensive, but having Trevor made things a bit easier for me. I couldn't wait to collect her.

She came running out and seemed very happy and couldn't wait to tell me what she had been doing all day. When the weekend came, she wanted to go to school on the Saturday. I had to explain that there was no school at the weekends. It was good that she settled in so well because there were no play schools in those days, so apart from playing with Sheila's little boy, David, she hadn't had contact with many children.

The school was about twenty minutes' walk from the flat, so doing that trip twice a day gave me my bit of exercise. I met some of the other mums and I am still in contact with two of them now. Linda did very well at school. The only thing that she had problems with was her sums. I blamed it on to the method of teaching; it was called the colour factor. They added up with colours, for example, red and green equalled a number. I have always been fairly good with figures, but I couldn't fathom it out. I feel sure that is why Linda was weak in that area. I spoke to a couple of other mums who had the same problem with their children.

My friend Maureen was having another baby and she asked me if I would look after Debra while she had it. I said I would. She was such a timid little girl. When I went to bath her she was very nervous. She only stayed for a few days but it worked out well; she settled in with Linda and Trevor. Maureen had another little girl and called her Alison.

Linda was going to have a medical at school and I was asked to be present. When the doctor examined her eyes, he said that there was a problem and he referred her to the school optician. I was told that she was very long sighted and needed strong glasses. It was all so quick and I was not very happy at the way that it was dealt with.

Dave and I discussed Linda's eyes and we decided we would get a second opinion. I took Linda to see my optician, who examined her eyes and said that he wouldn't make a decision. He referred her to the London Refraction Hospital for a specialist opinion. We got the appointment and Dave came with us.

Her eyes were examined and we were told that she did need glasses. The optician said that he didn't know how she had ever managed at school. We let her choose a frame herself, but wearing glasses really affected her, and I think the school children used to taunt her. Dave said to her, "What happened to my happy little girl?" We promised her that when she got older she could have contact lenses.

The firemen were good at organising things for the children. At Christmas they would have a party at the fire station, and organise a trip to a pantomime, which we all enjoyed. They would also get tickets for the circus when one came to town.

My cousin, Joyce, came to visit me and asked me if I would look after her little girl, Mandy, so that she could get a job, and I said I would. She was about three – a pretty little girl with bright red hair. Joyce used to arrive in a taxi to drop her off and collect her late in the afternoon. Mandy still had a dummy, but I managed to get it away from her gradually by playing a little game with her.

We had a little blow up paddling pool that we could put in the garden when the weather was warm the children loved to go in it. I used to sit out there with them. At least they were getting plenty of fresh air.

Veronica, Linda Trevor & Mandy in the garden of the flat 1963

In the summer after I took Linda to school, I would go home, do my housework, and then take the children to the common. There was a paddling pool and I used to meet my friends and their children.

It was a simple life but we were content. We didn't need a lot of money to enjoy ourselves. That is not to say that a bit more money wouldn't have been appreciated. I did get paid a bit for looking after Mandy, which I used to save until there was something that we needed.

I was at the paddling pool on the common one day, when Joyce turned up and started shouting and swearing at me. She said that Trevor had been getting at Mandy. He was only about three years old and they played together very well. I couldn't understand where she had got this idea from.

I went home very upset, and Dave wanted to know what was wrong. When I told him, he rushed up to the common and told Joyce that I wouldn't look after Mandy any more. He never liked anyone swearing at me. The next day, Joyce's man friend arrived at our flat and begged me to look after Mandy. At first I said no, but then I gave in. I had her that day and then I never saw any of them again.

I used to do a bit of knitting in the evenings. We had got a television by then but I still liked to have something to do. During the day I could always keep busy.

Dave did a bit of part time work for some extra money. There were a few firemen who delivered carpets for a local store, and he used to do that sometimes. We were out shopping one day, and we met up with someone called Ron who used to live in the same road as me when I was a child. Ron was a window cleaner, and he asked Dave if he would like to help him. He decided he would. He didn't earn a fortune, but it gave him a bit of pocket money for his pipe tobacco.

We decided to have another holiday at a holiday camp. It wasn't always possible to get away because Dave didn't have a choice of when he could take time off, and we didn't want Linda to miss school. This holiday camp was in Cromer, Norfolk, run by the same company as the one on the Isle of Wight. What we liked about these family camps was that there was no alcohol allowed and no bars. There was always plenty to do.

The beach was lovely, and we met some really nice people there, an older couple with their daughter and son-in-law. I kept in touch with Rene and Bill for years until they died. I am still in touch with their daughter, Maralyn, and her husband Barry.

One day, Trevor was playing outside with a cricket bat that Dave had made for him, when all of a sudden there was a very loud bang. He had smashed the glass back door. He ran indoors and locked himself in the bathroom and was then unable to unlock it. Dave had to get in through the bathroom window, which was very difficult. Trevor was so frightened – firstly by breaking the window and then by getting locked in.

Dave was on duty at Christmas that year. He left to start work at six in the evening. About an hour later I heard someone at the front door, and it was Dave. I was very surprised and wondered what was wrong. When I asked him, he said that there was one too many men on duty and no one else wanted to go home, so he jumped at the chance. It was lovely to have him home and the children were pleased.

When Dave got news that his dad had had an accident in his car, it prompted him to start having driving lessons, because he felt so helpless that he couldn't just pop down to see him. His dad wasn't seriously injured, but had whiplash. I knew that once Dave started to learn, he would want to buy a car. I never liked the thought of borrowing money to buy a car; I felt it was extravagant. We did have some money in our post office books and Dave used his for a deposit. He bought a little Morris Minor. It was a good little runner and although I wasn't very keen on the idea, it did get us around. I was always so thrifty, and I thought we would be living above our means.

I saw an advert in a local shop for someone to look after a little boy. He was about fifteen months old. His mum needed to work because her husband was at art school. She said that she would leave her little boy, Matthew, with me and see how he settled down.

Matthew was a dear little boy. He had blonde hair and was very fragile. He soon settled in and became one of the family, though at first he didn't seem to like Dave and he would cry when Dave came home from work.

Matthew

We were coming back from school one day when Trevor suddenly let go of Matthew's push chair and ran across the road. A driver had to make an emergency stop. I screamed because I thought he was going to get knocked down. I apologised to the driver and went home rather shaken up. I never relied on Trevor holding on to the pushchair again; instead I made him hold my hand.

The dustmen used to make a fuss of Trevor, and one day they gave him a football. I don't know if they had found it. He was always kicking a football around, and of course Dave loved that because he was very fond of sport. He used to box when he was at school and he liked running and swimming. He played volleyball to keep fit for his job.

We received a letter from my sister, Frances, asking if she, Morris and their two children, Andre and Lesley could come and stay for a few days. We only had the two bedrooms so it wasn't going to be easy. We had a single fold up bed and Mr Hicks, our neighbour, said that he would lend us a bed.

It all worked out very well, until one morning Frances said that Lesley had wet the bed, which was the one that Mr Hicks had lent us. I dreaded telling him, but he was really good about it.

Soon after that, I was in the kitchen doing my washing, when my neighbour upstairs, who had told me I could give her telephone number to use in an emergency, came to the door to tell me that my dad was on the phone. I went to her flat and spoke to him; he told me that my brother, Anthony, had died the day before.

It was the day before his fourteenth birthday, 1 October 1964. I found out that he'd had an asthma attack in the middle of the night. Apparently my mother had hidden his inhaler, because she thought he was using it too much. He got out of bed to look for it and collapsed. He was dead by the time the doctor arrived. I went to pieces when I got the news. My poor dad was devastated. The funeral was the following week on Linda's sixth birthday. I felt awful not being able to be with her on that day, but I felt I had to go to the funeral.

My dad and I decided to travel by coach to Margate, Kent, where my mum lived with her new husband, as it was cheaper to go by coach. I wasn't looking forward to seeing my mum; I hadn't seen her in a few years. Her husband said that he couldn't understand why none of her daughters wanted anything to do with her, but he didn't know what kind of life we had when we were children. I didn't travel very well on the coach and felt awful. It was a very sad funeral and I was glad to get home.

Chapter Eight

At the beginning of 1966, Dave came home from work and said that firemen were wanted in Reading, Berkshire, and he was thinking of applying. The money wasn't as good as it was in London, which came with a London weighting allowance, but he had never settled in London, being a country boy.

He went for an interview and was told that the job came with a new three bedroomed house. At the time they were not sure where it would be because there were three different sites: two at a place just outside Reading called Tilehurst, and the other a bit further away in Pangbourne. Dave got through the interview and was allocated a house in Tilehurst, which was three miles from Reading town.

I was a bit apprehensive about moving because a tied house didn't have as much security as a council property. We went to see the house and it was very nice. It was the middle of three. On one side there was an elderly couple, Mr and Mrs Noakes, and on the other side, a young couple, Jean and Eddie Moffet, who had just got married. They hadn't moved in yet because she wanted it furnished and carpeted first. She also wanted a telephone connected.

There were three bedrooms and a bathroom upstairs, a lounge and kitchen downstairs, an integral garage and a garden. There was an open fire in the lounge with a back boiler to heat the water, and an immersion heater as a backup. There was no central heating – that wasn't commonplace until the 1980s.

The houses were set back off the road and there was a side entrance to our garden, between Jean and Eddie's house and the house next door. That house also belonged to the fire brigade. The only thing that I didn't like in the house was that the exit to the garden was from the lounge, not the kitchen.

We moved in May. It was a bright and sunny day, and the children were very excited. I had mixed feelings about the move. I loved our flat, and I knew that I was going to miss my friends. It also meant that Linda would have to start a new school. It wasn't possible to get her into the local Catholic school, but the headmistress, Sister Anselm, said that as soon as she had a vacancy she would take Linda.

Before we moved we had found a medium size boy's bike. We put notices up to say that we found it, but no one ever came for it, so when we moved we took it with us. Trevor was only four and he used to take it to the end of our neighbours' drive, put his foot on a post that was there, and away he would go. Mr and Mrs Noakes used to watch him from their kitchen window.

One day, he was out riding the bike and he went right into a lamp post. John was at work and there was no easy way to get him to the hospital, so I asked Mr Noakes if he would take us. Trevor had to have stitches in his forehead, and I was so upset, which I was whenever he or Linda hurt themselves.

Linda was due to take her First Holy Communion when we moved. I bought her dress and veil. They didn't seem to make such a big thing of it in Reading as they did in London. We still had a nice day though.

Linda & Trevor

Linda started at the local school, Park Lane Primary, which was just at the top of the road, about five minutes away. There were several shops near the school: grocers, greengrocers, butchers, post office and newsagents. The doctor who we registered with was about fifteen to twenty minutes' walk away.

Once we moved into the house and unpacked, Dave set to and started digging the garden. It was hard work, especially when it was so hot. He planted some privet hedges between us and Jean and Eddie's garden. He wanted to grow vegetables, but kept a small grass patch and room for a few flowers.

About a week after we moved in to our house, Dave and I were in the kitchen when we noticed that there were flames coming out of the house opposite. He ran across the road and went into the house to search for anyone who might be still inside; luckily everyone had got out. The fire appliances arrived, but it was a bit scary, and it brought home what Dave did for a living.

Another fireman and his wife moved into the other house, and after two weeks they moved out as they couldn't settle. It made me wonder if we had done the right thing: it was a bit unsettling, but there was no going back.

When Dave was asked by the station officer how we were all settling in, he said we were fine. I never told him that I had mixed feelings about living there. It affected Trevor and me the most. Linda and Dave were really happy.

Now and again we used to go back to London to see Chris and Harry and some of my friends. My stomach used to get all knotted up, and I wished that we could turn the clock back. After a few months, my friend, Maureen, and her husband Mac and family came to visit us. I was telling her how I was feeling, and she said that she was the same when they moved from London to Banbury, in Oxfordshire. After our little chat, I was much better.

I saw an advert in a shop window for a bike for sale. I went to see it, and the lady had it hanging on the wall in her garage. She only wanted a pound for it, so I bought it. It had a little basket on the front, and I used it to do my shopping. I found it so useful and went everywhere on it.

Jean and Eddie moved in next door. Eddie sometimes used to work at night and Jean was frightened to be on her own, so she used to come and sit with us at our house. She was expecting a baby around Christmas time. I had got used to being on my own when Dave was on nights.

I managed to get myself a little cleaning job for one and a half hours twice a week. I went on my bike and Trevor rode his. It wasn't far to go, but it would have taken a lot longer if we had walked. The lady who I worked for was a German, Mrs Gubbins, and her husband had a shop selling motorcar spare parts. They had three little girls. It was a three-bedroom house, with two rooms and a kitchen downstairs, and Mrs Gubbins liked to be outside and was often working on her large garden.

I didn't earn a fortune, but it helped; I got five shillings an hour. Dave wasn't earning as much as he was in London. He didn't get the last pay rise before we moved, which he was expecting, and missed the added London allowance. He contacted the union rep in London about it, but he never heard back from him.

Later that year, I heard from Sister Anselm, that she had a place for Linda, and that she would take her in the New Year. I went to see her and told her that I could kiss her. She said, "Don't do that." Linda was very excited about going to the English Martyrs School. It was a bit further away, but only about fifteen to twenty minutes' walk. We would soon get into a routine. She was doing very well at Park Lane School; we had no complaints about it, but I wanted her to go to English Martyrs.

In September, my dad came to stay with us for a month. He had moved to Broadstairs, and was living with my sister, Pamela. He wasn't very happy. Pamela was with a married man, but he just kept her in a flat or house and didn't live with her. It was a funny sort of life, because if they wanted to go out anywhere, it always had to be somewhere that he wasn't known, in case his wife found out.

Dad enjoyed staying with us, and when he went back, I broke my heart. Dave said that I could have him come to live with us if I wanted him to, but it would have been a bit difficult with only having three bedrooms. I wouldn't have hesitated if we had the room.

On 16 December, I had just come home from seeing a nativity play at Linda's school. I was poking the fire, when there was a ring at the door. When I opened the door, there was a policeman standing there. He asked me if I was on my own, and I said I was, and that my husband was at a meeting. Before he said anything I thought that Dave might have been involved in an accident. He then said that he would like to come in. He told me that my dad was seriously ill. The policeman gave me a number to ring the hospital. He was in Chartham Hospital, Canterbury, Kent.

I was anxious for Dave to come home, but in the meantime I went next door to ask Jean and Eddie if I could use their phone to ring the hospital and give their phone number in case the hospital needed to contact me. They said I could. Dave came home and he could see that I was upset, so I told him the news. He tried to comfort me by putting his arms around me. At about two in the morning, there was a ring at our front door. Dave went down to answer it, and it was Jean, she said that there was a phone call from the hospital.

We went into Jean's house and I picked up the phone, the nurse told me that my dad had passed away. I broke down and Dave had to take the phone, because I wasn't taking anything in. The hospital that he was admitted to was for mentally ill patients. Apparently, when the doctor arrived to examine him, he asked to be transferred, stating that he was not mentally ill. He had shown similar symptoms to mental health patients because he was suffering from lack of oxygen to the brain.

Pamela went to pieces – she had always suffered with her nerves. Frances had just gone to Singapore with Morris. It just left me to go to Broadstairs and arrange the funeral. It was a difficult time, because it was only a week before Christmas. Chris said that she would look after the children for us.

I was having a tidy around the house before going to London, when I fell down the stairs with the hoover in my hand. Dave came rushing out from the kitchen and when he went to pick me up, I felt myself blacking out. I went upstairs to lie on the bed for a while, but soon got up, because I knew there was a lot to do before we left the next day.

We took the children to Chris in London and then Dave dropped me off at Victoria Station. I was unable to carry my case with my right hand, because my arm was so painful. It never occurred to me to go and be checked over at the doctor's or hospital. Dave had to go back to Reading but was going to get time off for the funeral, so would be travelling to Broadstairs later. I stayed with Pamela, but she was in no fit state to do anything. In fact, she wasn't even able to go to the funeral.

I had to let my youngest sister, Margaret, know that our dad had died. She was only fourteen and was heartbroken when I told her. It was the first time that I had seen my mum since Anthony's funeral. I think that when Anthony died my dad gave up. He couldn't get over losing his only son.

Margaret

The funeral was on 22 December. It didn't register at the time, but it was my mum's birthday. I was very upset when I went to the undertakers, because I found out that my mum had never paid for Anthony's funeral. I just couldn't believe it! I assured the undertaker that I would settle the account for my dad's funeral.

There were not many people at the funeral. My dad didn't have any friends in Broadstairs, and with Frances and Pamela not being there, there weren't many relatives. I did manage to get hold of his brother, George. He had one other brother who was still alive and a sister, but I didn't know how to contact them.

Dave and I asked Pamela if she would like to come back with us for a few days and she said yes. We travelled to London the next day to collect the children. While we were there, I went to the hospital where my dad had worked as a storeman. The staff were shocked to hear about my dad and said what a lovely man he was and how they missed him. He had been medically retired since the May of that year. He wasn't a lazy man; but he couldn't work any longer. He used to get so out of breath, because he suffered with emphysema, probably caused by smoking.

After thanking Chris for looking after the children, we returned to Reading. It was a very quiet Christmas, but we did the best that we could for the sake of the children. I kept shedding a few tears when thinking about my dad and I would walk around the shops in a bit of a daze. Trevor said, "Granddad was going to take me on a plane." He was a bit too young to understand. Pamela started to get a bit restless and wanted to go home, so Dave took her part of the way and her John met them and took her home from there.

Chapter Nine

At the beginning of 1967, I decided to try and get a part time job, with more hours than the cleaning job, as Trevor would be starting school soon.

I had managed to get Trevor into the same school as Linda, English Martyrs. On his first day, I felt terrible having to leave him. We were both very upset. It was so different from Linda's first day at school; she was a lot more studious, and as soon as she was able to read she always had her head in a book.

I decided that I had to be cruel to be kind, and I told him that he wouldn't get any sweets until he went to school without any fuss. It seemed to do the trick. He never found going to school easy. When Dave and I went to an open evenings, the teacher said that it was as if he was in a shell. When I look back I think he took after me, because I always felt insecure when I was at school.

I wanted more for my children than my poor level of education. I always made sure that they went to school; they had to be really unwell for me to keep them at home. Linda was fortunate that she didn't have any health problems. Trevor coped very well with his asthma; it was something that he was going to have to learn to live with.

Once I knew that Trevor was more settled in school (he was never going to like it as much as Linda) I started to look for a job. I got an interview for a bought ledger clerk. I had never done that kind of work before, but thought I would give it a try. I had done ledger work, but this was different.

I was offered the job with part time hours that suited me. It would enable me to take the children to school before I started. Once I had finished my job, I could go home, do my jobs, prepare a meal, then go and meet the children from school. I wasn't looking forward to telling Mrs Gubbins that I couldn't do her cleaning anymore, but I discovered she was expecting it, and understood. She said, "I was dreading this day. I thought that once Trevor started school, you would want to get a job with more hours."

The firm I was going to work for was a mineral water company, Apex Juices, in Wilton Road, Reading. They also sold some wines and spirits and delivered mainly to public houses.

Because Dave worked shift work, our meals were planned around them. When he was on day duty his hours were nine until six, and when he was on nights they were six until nine. We would have our meal when he got home from day duty, and before going out when he was on nights. I never wanted Dave to have warmed up meals, and it was nice to eat together as a family. It was different if there was a call out just before his shift ended – then I had no choice.

I started my new job and soon got into the swing of it. I really enjoyed it. One of the partners, Mr Raymont, worked in the office and the other one, Mr Robinson, worked in the factory. I would prepare the accounts through to payments. I would then present them to Mr Robinson, and he would tell me who and what amount I could pay. He rarely paid an account in full, especially the big companies. Once he had approved them, I would write out the cheques and leave them on his desk for signature.

There was another lady in the office who did the sales ledger called Mrs Treacher. She was a very hard person to get on with. I think she was a very unhappy person in her personal life and didn't get on with her husband. They seemed to live separate lives in the same house. I found it very strange.

The conditions in the office and around were pretty awful, but I stuck it out because the hours suited me. I was there for a few years. There were not many part time jobs about at that time. There was only one toilet for the factory and the office. I hated going in there because it was never clean.

There were ladies in the factory that used to peel onions all day, ready for pickling. They got paid a pittance but still turned up every day.

I saw a job advertised for a bought ledger clerk for more money and I decided to apply for it. I was told at the beginning of the interview that they had several people to see, so was very surprised when I was offered the job. When I went to work the next day, I plucked up courage to tell my boss I had been offered another job with more money, and if he matched it I would stay. He did, so I turned the offer down. Mrs Treacher wasn't very happy about me getting more money. I was pleased I didn't take the other job as some months later there was a big fire in the building where I would have been working, so I would have been out of work.

I started to get a lot of pain in my hands. I noticed it especially when I was writing. My fingers were going white as well. The doctor diagnosed Raynaud's syndrome and told me to make sure that I was warm before going out in the cold. It is a disorder of the blood vessels in which exposure to the cold causes the small arteries to contract suddenly. This action cuts off blood flow to the digits, which become pale. The fingers on both hands are usually affected, and sometimes the toes. I accepted what the doctor told me and hoped that it would improve.

I was due for some time off work and I found that my hands were a bit better during my break. Once I went back to work I was back to square one. Things didn't improve, so I went back to see the doctor. He referred me to the local hospital to see an orthopaedic surgeon, Mr Squires.

After being examined and having an x-ray on my neck, Mr Squires told me that at some time I had broken a bone in my neck. I asked him if it could have happened when I fell down the stairs. He said that that was probably when it had happened, but he didn't think that it was what was causing the pain that I was experiencing. He decided to get me fitted with a collar – the one thing that I was dreading – to see if it would help.

I had to go back after a month, and things were no better. I hated wearing the collar, as people kept asking me what I had done. Most people assume that you have been in some kind of motor accident when they see you wearing a collar. Mr Squires suggested I had an operation to pull my shoulders back because I am round shouldered. I decided to see if things improved. It was a big operation and it would have been permanent.

After several months, I went back to see my doctor and he referred me to a specialist in London, at the Hospital for Nervous Diseases. The specialist said that there was nothing that he could do for me. He implied it was all in my mind. In the middle of talking to me, he fell asleep at his desk. When he woke up, he said that he would ask my doctor to prescribe some antidepressants.

This was something that I didn't want, but I was willing to give it a try. I didn't think it would solve the problem because I didn't feel that I was depressed; it was a physical problem, but a difficult one to diagnose. I always thought that it had something to do with me falling down the stairs, because I was all right before that happened.

When Linda was nine, she decided she wanted to join the Red Cross, so one evening I took her to enrol in a little hut where the meetings were held. It was about a fifteen-minute walk from where we lived. She loved to go and soon made a lot of friends. Once she had been going for a while, someone would give her a lift home, which was very helpful.

I got friendly with some neighbours over the road, Audrey and Jim. They had three sons, Stephen, Kevin and David. David used to make me laugh, because if Audrey sent him across to our house with a message, he would have forgotten it before he arrived. He was and is a very likeable person. I had to go into hospital for a little bowel operation and Audrey came to visit me. I thought it was very nice, because I hadn't known her very long, but then she is that sort of a person, always out to help anyone.

After a few days, I was transferred to a convalescent hospital, which wasn't far from where we lived. Trevor was fretting because I wasn't at home, and his asthma was bad. Dave asked at the hospital if he could bring him to visit me, and was told that he could. When he walked down the ward and saw me, his little face lit up and then he was all right. I was soon home after that.

Around that time, Linda made her Confirmation, and she looked lovely in her white dress and veil.

Linda's Confirmation   Linda, Trevor & a neighbour

Chapter Ten

1969 wasn't a very good year. Dave's Aunt Win became very ill. We were on our way to visit her, when our car broke down. We hadn't had it very long. There was a terrible noise and it felt like the car had collapsed. We were in Calne, in Wiltshire. The police turned up and took one look at me and said that I was in shock. They took me into someone's house, and they made me a cup of tea. Dave had to hire a car so that we could continue the journey. It was just before the final part of the M4 motorway opened up, so it took a lot longer to get to Wales. When we arrived at the hospital, Aunt Win was very poorly. She couldn't speak because the doctors had performed a tracheotomy to help her breathe, and so she had to write things down. It was very sad to see her.

It wasn't long after that she died and we went back for the funeral. We met her adopted son, George. There weren't many people at the funeral. We went to the church service and then only the men were allowed to go to the crematorium. She never had much of a life, but then not a lot of people did at that time. Housework was hard work, as there were no labour saving devices to help working class people.

Dave and I were going to book a holiday in a holiday camp in Devon, and when Audrey found out, she asked if we would mind if she and her family came. It snowballed and Uncle George and Aunt Georgina came as well. We were winning all the prizes. We had a lovely time with lots of things to do and plenty going on. Dave entered a competition for knobbly knees. I entered one for lovely ankles and was amazed when I won it. It was at a time when miniskirts were in fashion, and I must say that I had a couple of short skirts – not too short though.

Dave having his knees felt   Dave & Veronica

During the year I suggested to some of our neighbours that we have a night out together. I would make all the arrangements and collect money on a weekly basis, to make it easier on the evening. There was a place called 'The Chicken in The Basket' where they had dinner and dance evenings. Even though I had reached the grand old age of thirty-two, I had never eaten out in a restaurant before. The evening was a great success and we went back again later. I have always enjoyed organising things.

Later on that year in October, Harry passed away very suddenly. Once again we got a message through our neighbours, Jean and Eddie. When I spoke to Chris, she said, "Please don't feel sorry for me." The only person to be very upset was Trevor. Dave didn't have any feelings for him. He never spent a lot of time under the same roof, because he was in the Navy. We went to London for the funeral and I thought I would shed a few tears, but I didn't.

The same year, we also had a letter from a distant relative of Miss Lloyd, to say that she had passed away. We weren't told in time to be able to go to her funeral, and we were a bit upset about that. She had a very lonely life in her one bedroom flat in Stockwell, London.

Even in those days, she was a bit nervous about living alone, and had a spy hole on her front door. I found it a bit worrying. I had never experienced anything like that before. We used to visit her when we could. We didn't know that she had any relatives, as nobody ever came to see her when we lived in the same house as her in Clapham. People always seem to come out of the woodwork when someone dies.

She thought the world of Linda. I suppose it was because she was around her for the first few years of her life. Linda often used to go upstairs to visit with her. She never married so I suppose she enjoyed taking an interest in the children. I don't know if she ever had a man in her life at any time. She never spoke of anyone.

In 1970, after having an arteriogram, to check if there were any blockages in my arteries, I was referred to another hospital in London and I was told that my problems with my hands could be caused by the fact that I had an extra rib. Arrangements were made for me to be admitted to hospital for the removal of my top right rib. I was then given another arteriogram, where I passed out. When I came around, I had had the operation to remove my rib.

The surgeon didn't seem to think that my fall down the stairs had anything to do with the symptoms that I was having. Things didn't improve. After several months I went back and saw the surgeon. There was a big meeting with lots of doctors and me. They asked me lots of questions; I was a bit of a mystery. Although I didn't have all the symptoms of carpel tunnel syndrome, (it is a tunnel that nerves run through in your hand) they decided to operate, to try and remove the pressure. I knew that it really was only trial and error.

I had the operation, and at first things seemed to improve, but I think it was just the fact that I wasn't using my hand very much. I was finding it very difficult to write and decided to leave my job.

Linda sat her eleven plus that year and we were anxiously waiting for the results. When we heard that she had passed, we were over the moon. Linda's choice of school was St Joseph's Convent in Reading. As a treat we took her to see Gilbert O'Sullivan in London. Linda was very fond of him and had some of his records. We made a day of it and had a meal in a restaurant afterwards.

We had to buy the uniform from a special shop, and it was very expensive. Some of the girls wore a cape in the winter and they looked lovely. We couldn't afford to buy a new cape, so I went to one of the uniform sales at the school with Linda and we managed to get one. It looked really great and we were very proud of her. It was a long journey to school for her, but it was worth it.

She had always devoted herself to her schooling. I always encouraged her to learn because of my lack of knowledge. I never expected her to help around the house, but looking back perhaps that was one mistake I made, because I realise now that it helps one later in life. I should have encouraged her to be more involved with domestic things, but I didn't want my children to have the kind of life that I had. I wanted them to enjoy their young years. You do the best you can as parents; there is no right or wrong way of doing things, and I'm sure that every parent has some regrets.

Chris and John called to see us unexpectedly. Chris was bursting to tell us that she and John were going to move to Tilehurst. She said that she wouldn't be on our doorstep, but would be nearby. We were very pleased for them and the children were very excited. At the time, John's job took him all around the country, so he was away for long periods, sometimes days.

The move went ahead and we were invited to see the new house. It was a semi-detached house in a cul-de-sac. It had three bedrooms and a bathroom upstairs, a lounge diner and kitchen downstairs, with a big garden and a detached garage.

After a short while, Chris was feeling unwell. John never told us what was wrong. He came and asked us if we could have her to stay with us for a while because his job was taking him away. The doctor called to see her at our house, but still we didn't know what her illness was. Once she went home, I would go and visit her on my bike after I got home from work. The neighbours thought I was the district nurse. She was always pleased to see me. There was never anything for me to do because John was so organised that he did everything before he went out in the morning.

She was taken into hospital but didn't seem to be improving. Linda used to call into see her on her way home from school. Chris loved to see her and regarded her as her own grandchild. Eventually she went home. John did all he could to make life more comfortable for her. He set up an intercom at the front door. A very kind neighbour kept an eye on her while John was at work, and used to take her some soup.

Chris passed away on 9 May 1971. The funeral was a very sad occasion; she was only sixty. Everyone who attended expressed concerned about how John would cope on his own, but he was very resilient. He had always been with his mum and he idolised her, but he just continued with his life the best he could.

Chapter Eleven

Audrey, Jim, Dave and I, would go out for a meal now and again, and Uncle George and Aunt Georgina would also join us at times.

From left Aunt Georgina, Audrey, Jim, Veronica and Dave

From left Jim, Veronica & Dave (with his lovely smile)

Trevor came home from school one day and said that he had been chosen by the parish priest to be an altar boy. I thought it was an honour, but I don't think he was very keen. It meant getting up early in the morning, something that he wasn't very good at. Sometimes the priest would ring to see if he was on his way. Trevor also started to play football for the school, and Dave was pleased that he had been chosen.

Linda played hockey at school and she also played tennis. Sometimes she would play with Trevor and he nearly always beat her. She said it wasn't fair because he hadn't had any tuition. Trevor had always been a natural sportsman. He also played cricket for the county and did high jump in athletics. He had gone to the local swimming baths with our neighbours and their children when he was about 5, and he taught himself to swim.

I applied for a job at the local butchers serving the customers. It was all day Thursday, Friday and Saturday morning. There was one other applicant, but she only wanted one day, so the butcher told us to sort it out ourselves. She decided that she would not go for it, so I got the job and I really enjoyed it. It was nice to meet people.

There was one elderly lady who I got friendly with whose name was Mrs Ransom. I worked there for quite a few months, but I was having a lot of pain in my hands and arms. I had been going to see an osteopath for treatment, and when I told her what I did, I was advised to leave. She said lifting the heavy joints in the cold wasn't helping my condition. The butchers were sorry to see me go, but I had to think of my health.

Mrs Ransom was upset and said that she would miss me. I told her that I would visit her if she gave me her phone number and address. We became good friends. She was in her late eighties and had one son, Bill, who had been divorced for years and then remarried someone called Jane. He had one daughter, Veronica. I tried to visit Mrs Ransom once a week, but it depended on Dave's shifts, because I wouldn't leave the children by themselves.

One day when I was visiting her and we were having a chat, she asked me if I would like a little drink. I said, "Yes please," and she produced a bottle of

Grand Marnier from a hiding place under the stairs. It became a regular thing when I went to visit. I had never tried it before and wasn't sure if I would like it, but I did and she enjoyed having a drink with me. I didn't have far to go home and at that time I didn't drive, so I didn't have to worry about drinking and driving.

Bill died very suddenly and Mrs Ransom never got over it. I was there when she had to tell her granddaughter. It was a very sad occasion. Eventually she went to live up north with her daughter-in-law.

At Christmas I would collect her and take her to our house for dinner. She loved asparagus, and at that time you could only buy it in season, but I managed to get a tin. She enjoyed being with the children, and they were very good with her. It was nice to be able to help an elderly lady have a good Christmas Day.

Trevor went to the Boy Scouts group one day, but he didn't like it and never went again. We thought we would see how he got on before spending money on a uniform. He never really said why he didn't like it. He got himself a paper round to earn some pennies. In those days he was a proper little miser. He didn't like to spend his money. He would buy a few sweets and save the rest. I used to worry that he would grow up being miserly. I needn't have worried; he changed as he got older.

Linda never bothered to get a job, she just managed with the little bit of pocket money that we gave her. She would rather have her head in a book. I would find her reading nearly every time I popped my head around her bedroom door in the morning. She certainly didn't take after me. Her dad used to read a lot at one time.

Dave and I were very fond of big band music, especially Glen Miller. There used to be concerts at the town hall at times and we would go if we could get tickets. At one show Dave requested they play 'The String of Pearls'. He knew that was my favourite. I have seen 'The Glen Miller Story' about four times.

After leaving the butcher's shop I got an afternoon job on the till at a cash and carry warehouse. I had never been very keen to work in the afternoon, as it made it more difficult to work around Dave's shifts.

Customers used to come with their trolleys and a member of staff would call out the code for the item and then the price. It was a big responsibility, but a person working in the office told me that my till was always accurate.

Once again, I saw a job advertised for someone to work in a café. It was attached to a driving school. I felt my previous experience working in a restaurant as a waitress when I was young might help me get the job. It did. I really enjoyed working at the café and meeting the public. When we weren't busy, I would clean the shelves down and the boss liked that.

There was one customer who had just got a pay out from the government. I think it was a pension from the war. He wanted to give my colleague and me some money. I think it was £10 each. We said we didn't want it, but he insisted. We said that we would have to clear it with our boss first. He was all right about it and so we accepted. We thought it was very kind of him.

One day, I was having a conversation with my work colleague who suggested I learn to drive. I said, "You must be joking. I'm a terrible passenger." When I got home, I thought about it some more, discussed it with Dave, and decided to give it a try. I didn't think in a million years that I would ever be any good. At the end of my first lesson, although I'd been very nervous, the instructor said that I had done well. He said that my steering was very good and that some people found it difficult.

After having nine lessons, I felt that I wasn't progressing, so Dave said that he would take me out. He was very patient with me and taught me a lot. I was dreading my test. I had the chief examiner, and he was awful. Needless to say, I failed. After a few weeks I took it again. I couldn't believe it when the same examiner came out. This time I passed, but I was very surprised because he was on at me all the time. Dave was waiting for me when I came out from the test centre, and he was so pleased when I told him that I had passed. It opened up a new world for me.

My first full driving licence 18 May 1973

Trevor broadened his horizons with his football: as well as playing for his school team he went on to play for a local boys' team. He progressed from the Reading under elevens to under fifteens. The manager said that he had the potential to be a professional, but he got fed up with it. He went for coaching to a place called Bisham Abbey; which is a well-known training place. The boys went there for a week. I think there were some fun and games that went on during that week, and I don't think Trevor was an angel.

Dave and I used to take him to all the matches. If Dave was on duty, then I would take him. We would call in at the fire station to let him know how the match went. My driving skills came in useful.

Bobby Williams (Manager) One of the lads with his Dad

Caversham Football team - Trevor left in back row

Linda got friendly with an elderly neighbour who had a little dog called Susan. She used to get off the bus and the dog would be waiting for her. When we got to know this man a bit better, I would collect him some Sundays and take him back to our house for dinner. As usual, I felt sorry for him. He had a son but hardly ever saw him. After some time Linda stopped calling in to see him. I wondered why but when I asked her, she never really answered me. I have wondered since if he had done something that he shouldn't have, or did something to embarrass her.

We used to have some lovely evenings when Dave was off duty: we would sit around the fire making toast and putting dripping on it. It was a simple and old-fashioned thing, but very enjoyable.

Dave's dad loved it at Tilehurst, and if we were on holiday he and Elsie would come and stay at our house. Once he came and stayed a few days on his own. Elsie hinted that he would like to live with us when he retired. Sadly he became ill soon after he retired in 1974. I remember speaking to him on the phone and his voice sounded awful. The next time I spoke to Elsie, she said that he had been diagnosed with cancer of the throat. He used to smoke a pipe; just like Dave. It was thought that smoking probably caused it. We used to visit when we could and saw him deteriorate.

By this time I had applied for another job – a messenger in the Civil Service. I had the interview and when I hadn't heard anything for a few weeks, I decided to ring them. The person who I spoke to said, "If you are the lady who had TB in 1955, you've got the job." I was given a starting date and told that I would receive confirmation in the post.

I waited but the letter never came. I received a phone call one Monday morning and was told that I should have been there that morning. When I said that I hadn't received the letter, I was asked if I could start the next morning instead, and I said I could.

I was going to work part time from eight until one, and so I caught the bus with Linda, although she had further to travel. Even though my title was messenger, I had to sit at a little desk at the entrance to the building. I had to open up in the mornings and it was my job to check the passes of the staff or any workmen.

The government rented parts of three different offices in Reading. The main building was Fountain House where all the post used to be delivered. We had the third to the sixth floors there. The department was called 'Intervention Board for Agriculture Produce', or IBAP. It was the new Common Market Department, and had been started a few months before I went to work there.

We dealt with all the subsidies given to farmers. There were numerous schemes, for example, grain, butter, milk, peas and beans. There were always new schemes opening up: one of them was called set-aside, where farmers were given money for not growing anything on their land. As a messenger, I had to move papers around from office to office, or for external items, to the post room in Fountain House.

My job got a bit boring at times, so I would take something to read. I was being well paid so I didn't complain. There was one member of staff who thought my job was too easy. She had a word with the senior messenger, and suggested that I did a couple of the runs with work that had to be taken to the post room. This didn't bother me; it made the time go quicker.

When I went for my interview, I mentioned that I had a two-week holiday booked. I was told that it would be honoured. When the time came I was more than surprised to find out that I would be paid. Your leave started at a certain time, usually the month of your birthday. You were given a leave sheet, with your entitlement written at the top. When you wanted to apply for leave, you checked the dates with your line manager, and then entered it on the sheet, deducting the number of days from the balance, and getting your line manager to sign it off.

One day I overheard someone talking about a system being installed where staff could gain entrance to the building by using a code. I spoke to the senior messenger, because I was a bit concerned that I might lose my job. Then I received a phone call from a senior officer, who had been at my interview, assuring me that my job was safe.

After the new system was installed, I moved from the entrance to join the messengers on the second floor. We used to go around the floors about once every hour to collect the post, also to distribute any that had come in. Getting to know the staff made the job a lot more interesting.

Dave was very pleased that I had got a secure job in the Civil Service. He said at least I would get a pension when I retired. I had never had a job like it before. It was a non-contributory pension, but later on changed, so that you had to contribute for a spouse.

I hadn't been at my new job for long, when Trevor got chicken pox very badly. I had to call the doctor in; he didn't want to come at first, but I told him that his asthma was a lot worse. When he came, he said it was the worst case of chicken pox that he had ever seen, and gave him some antibiotics for his chest. There isn't any treatment for chickenpox. You just have to put calamine lotion on to try and soothe it. Soon after, Linda went down with it; but thankfully she didn't have it as badly.

I don't know what made him start, but Trevor began to collect sachets and cubes of sugar. I used to get quite a lot from my colleagues who went abroad for their holidays, so he got quite a collection. In 1974, there was a shortage of sugar and when the shops got some in customers were only allowed to have one packet. The news used to get around at work like lightning, and the staff would rush out to get some. Needless to say Trevor wouldn't let us have any of his!

Chapter Twelve

Linda came home from school one day and said that she had been made head girl. We were very proud of her, as it was quite an honour. She always looked smart when she went to school. She wore her uniform until she left school, and she was nearly nineteen.

In October 1974, my sister, Pamela was getting married. My uncle rang me and told me she was marrying a man who had nine children. He is a Kenyan Asian, his wife had died and Pamela went to help him. A relationship developed and they decided to get married. I was a bit surprised because she had been with a married man for years, but evidently that relationship was now over.

We received an invitation to the wedding. I wasn't sure if I wanted to go, because I knew my mum would be there. We talked about it and Trevor said that he would like to meet his nan. I felt then that we should make an effort. Linda and I went to London to buy something for her to wear to the wedding. We bought a green cape and trousers to match. It looked lovely on her, setting off her strawberry blonde hair. While we were in London, we went to see the show, 'Fiddler on The Roof'. It was really good and we both enjoyed it.

I wasn't looking forward to going to the wedding, but it all went off well. It was a big affair, a white wedding with several bridesmaids. We saw my mum, who was pleased to see the children. It was two days before Linda's birthday, and Mum promised to send her something. I told Linda not to bank on it. I was right; she didn't even get a card.

Pamela & Claude 1974

Dave had been on night duty the night before, so at the end of the evening he was very tired and I had to drive home. We had just left Broadstairs, when we heard on the radio that there had been a bombing in Guildford, so we had to make a detour to get home.

We were all very tired when we got home. Dave and I wondered what Pamela had taken on. It was going to be very hard bringing up nine children, and the youngest was only a baby.

We used to have some good parties at our house. Some of the neighbours came, even Mr Noakes, who seemed to let his hair down and really enjoyed himself. His wife never joined us, as she didn't like parties. Uncle George and Auntie Georgina came once. I can still hear him singing, 'Knock three Times on The Ceiling'. He was such a loving person. Some of Dave's mates from work came too. I did all the catering and one of Dave's mate's wives congratulated me on how well everything was presented. I liked to keep all the food covered up until it was time to eat, as it kept it fresh.

From left, Uncle George Veronica Dave behind Aunt Georgina, Jim & Audrey

Linda seemed to be down in the dumps. When we asked her what was wrong, she said that it wasn't fair that some of the girls in her class seemed to get everything they wanted. We had to explain that we weren't in the same league as their parents. Most of the girls at the convent were there privately. We reminded her that she got there on her own merit.

The endowment that we had been paying into since she was born was due to mature, so we said that she could have her contact lenses. That cheered her up. She had to learn that some people have more material things than others, but the most important things in life are good food, health, and love. I think our children had all of these things.

Once Linda got her lenses, it made a great difference to her confidence. We could see the change in her. It took her a while to get used to them. At first she got herself all worked up when she was trying to put them in. I think she did very well. I don't think I could have coped with them.

About this time, Linda was busy studying for her O levels. She really worked hard and did most of it on her own. I was unable to help her. It was all above my head. Apart from the fact that I had missed so much schooling, things had changed so much. Her dad used to help her where he could.

One year, Linda, Trevor and I went to London to see an ice show. The church had arranged it. When we got there, I bought a programme and there was a prize of a bike for the person who bought the one with a lucky number. When the winner was announced, we looked at our number and it was the next one up from ours. We almost got it. Linda wrote about the trip for the church magazine.

Trevor used to go to the local park with his mates. They formed a bike speedway. If any of the bikes got smashed up, he would repair them. What I didn't know was that he was using bits of my old bike to do his repairs. I don't know if he received any money for the repairs that he did.

Linda received her O Level results and got very good grades. We were all so proud of her.

Chapter Thirteen

Linda had a pen friend who lived in Austria. She had been writing to her for some time before she asked us if she could go to visit her. We couldn't afford to pay for her to fly, so we said that we would pay her train fare, but she would have to save for her spending money.

It was a worrying time knowing that she would be travelling on her own. We took her to Victoria station and made sure that she got the right train. We had a rough idea what time she would be arriving in Vienna, and I had a phone number to ring. I was like a cat on hot bricks until I knew that she was all right, and was so relieved to hear her voice. She was going to spend a month with Gerda and her family.

While Linda was away, Dave, Trevor and I went to the Isle of Wight for two weeks. We couldn't get into the same guest house for the two weeks, so we went to two different ones. The second one was the best. We were the only people there. We had two lovely weeks, and the weather was very kind to us.

We were looking forward to Linda coming home; it seemed funny without her. When she came home, she was surprised to see how brown we all were from our holiday. She said that it looked as if we had been abroad.

We discovered that she didn't get on all that well with Gerda, and they had nothing in common. We thought that she would have known that before she went, because she had been writing to her for such a long time. The arrangement was that Gerda would come on a return visit the following year.

That year Linda started to learn to drive. She had some lessons and then Dave took her out a few times, but in the end he gave up. He said that she wasn't easy to teach, so I used to go with her sometimes. She failed the first three tests and Dave said we weren't going to pay for her to do any more. I talked him into letting her have one more, because I said that it would be such a waste of our money otherwise. I am pleased to say that she passed the fourth time. Her boyfriend, Ian, also took four tests before he passed.

For two or three years, I had been going to The Fire Brigade Conference with Dave. Our friends Audrey and Jim looked after the children for us. Linda and Trevor came with us one year, because Linda was interested in politics.

From left, Linda, Dave, Trevor and Veronica

One of our neighbour's daughters, Cynthia, was making an evening dress for me to wear at one of the functions at conference. She lived on a farm, and I went with Dave and Trevor to have a fitting one evening. Cynthia came in with a little puppy. It was a border collie; a lovely rusty colour. He looked a bit like a fox.

Dave fell in love with it. He had always wanted a dog, and so had Linda. I had never been that keen, and although we had a dog called Bonzo when I was a child, he was a bit of a liability, out of control and never taken for a walk.

Of course, we ended up having this puppy. We called him Rex. We had to go and pick Linda up from Red Cross, and when she got in the car she was so excited when she saw the new member of the family sitting on the back seat with Trevor. I was still not sure about him.

Our friend Audrey looked after him when I was at work and Dave wasn't around. He was a bit of a handful, and it was me who got landed with taking him for a walk when Dave wasn't there. I even had to get out of my bed to take him for a walk one evening after having a migraine. I wasn't very happy.

Linda with Rex

I was nervous around him, and he knew it. One evening when Dave was on night duty, he jumped up onto the settee. I told him to get down, and he just snarled at me. When Dave came home the next morning, I said, "If the dog doesn't go, I will." Audrey and Jim couldn't understand how Dave couldn't see what Rex was doing to me.

Dave went to a local place that re-homed animals and someone agreed to take him. A few days later we got a phone call asking if we would take him back, because he had frightened the person who had taken him. Needless to say, we didn't have him back, and we don't know what happened to him.

Later on that year Dave's dad got a lot worse. We went to see him and he looked awful. He was a man of few words, but I remember him looking at Dave and saying, "You've got a good one there, look after her." Dave said, "I will." It brought tears to my eyes. I don't think he had had a very happy life.

I arranged to have a few days off work to go to Winkton near Christchurch, Dorset, which was where Dave's dad and Elsie lived. Audrey said that she would keep an eye on the children when Dave was at work. I drove myself, and Dad and Elsie were pleased to see me. I helped out in general around the house, doing some of the things that Elsie had let go because of looking after Dad. I kept an eye on Dad when Elsie went out. He spent most of his time in bed.

One night after I had gone to bed, I heard Dad scream out. I went into his bedroom and he was holding his head because he was in so much pain. I said to Elsie that she should phone for the doctor. I didn't think that he should be suffering like that. She said that the doctor would just say that he had his medication. It was quite clear that he was in terrible pain. Elsie did call the doctor, and when he came he gave him an injection. After that he went to sleep, so Elsie and I went back to bed.

When it was time for me to go home, Dad didn't want me to go. On the way home, I felt very upset and shed a few tears. I had to try and take my mind off things because I had such a long drive home. I wished we lived a bit nearer, so that we could help out more.

At the beginning of 1976 we had a phone call from Elsie, to say that Dad had been taken to hospital in Poole, Dorset. Dave and his brother went to visit him. A few days later, John took me. We would stay at the hospital all day. It was clear that Dad wasn't getting any better.

We went back home and then Elsie rang to tell us that Dad had been moved to a new hospice that had recently opened in Christchurch. A couple of weeks later Dave and I went to see him, and Dave walked past his bed, because he didn't recognise him. When we went outside, I was very upset after seeing him and I told Dave that I didn't want to see him anymore; he looked so awful.

Dad passed away in February. Even though we were expecting it, it was still a shock. We went to the funeral and, apart from the family, there were several of his friends from the Water Board where he used to work. I broke down on the way to the crematorium. I was so upset as he was only sixty-nine and hardly had any quality time after he retired. Life can be so cruel at times.

Chapter Fourteen

Dave got tickets to see Manchester City play Newcastle in The Milk Cup, and Trevor, Dave and I went to Wembley to watch them play. I had never been to a big match before, and never Wembley. We went on a coach and when we arrived at the coach park, we didn't take much notice of what was around us.

We were standing with the Newcastle supporters but supporting Manchester City. When they scored we cheered, and people near us gave us dirty looks. It was a great day and quite an experience. When it was time to go back to the coach, Dave said, "Keep close to me." I found it all a bit overwhelming. We eventually made our way back to the coach park, but couldn't find ours for a long time. We were the last ones back and everyone on board was singing, 'Why are we waiting'.

1976 was a very hot summer. It got hot in April and went through to October. Gerda was coming to visit and it wasn't the best time for her to come to England, because everything was so dried up. Unlike Linda when she went to Austria, Gerda came by plane. It wasn't too far to the airport for us to pick her up.

We made her as welcome as we could. It was sometimes a bit difficult because she didn't understand everything that we were saying. It soon became clear Linda was right: they didn't have a lot in common.

It was difficult to know what to do every day for a month. It was a long time to keep someone occupied and interested in things. We did our best and took her out to several places. Trevor got on very well with her, and used to talk with her a lot. John very kindly took them out a couple of times, once to Stratford-on-Avon.

Trevor with Gerda

from left, Linda Veronica & Gerda

I usually like the heat, but it was beginning to get to me. I would get home from work, do my chores, prepare the dinner, and then I wouldn't feel like doing much else, so I would sit in the garden when it was nice, but it was even too hot to enjoy that.

Veronica & Dave July 1976

In 1977 Linda was getting ready to do three A level exams. It kept her very busy and she used to get a bit up tight. I would tell her to have a break and go for a walk. It was a lot of pressure.

This year I celebrated my fortieth birthday, and Audrey, Jim, Dave and I went to a pub in Caversham to have a meal. Dave got talking to the Proprietor, who said that he and his wife were celebrating their silver wedding anniversary that day. They invited us to stay for a drink after the pub closed. We had a very enjoyable evening.

Dave and I were planning to go on holiday to Wales in August. Trevor and one of his friends, Kevin, were coming with us. They wanted to take their bikes, but Dave wasn't very keen. He gave in eventually. We were going to stay in a caravan that was in someone's garden. We had been there before with Linda and had a good time.

Linda was going camping with the Red Cross. They were taking disabled children. I think it was hard work, but she liked that sort of thing. I arranged my time off work and was looking forward to the break. The day came and Dave secured the bikes on top of the car. Soon after we arrived at the caravan, the boys went off on their bikes and Dave and I went for a walk.

We had a lovely week, spending some time on the beach, and Dave and I did some walking. The weather was kind to us. We got friendly with an elderly man who lived in a bungalow. I think we just saw him outside his home and we started talking to him. His name was Mr Williams. His garden was very overgrown, because he was unable to do it anymore. Dave told him that if we lived nearer, he would do it for him; he was very kind like that. Our holiday over, we were back home and back to work. I never minded going back to work because I enjoyed what I did.

The next thing was to wait for Linda's exam results. When they came, she was nervous about opening them. She needn't have been, because she passed them all with good grades. She would now be able to go to Aberystwyth University and read law; that was her first choice and it was the university that Prince Charles attended.

Dave was at a union meeting when her results arrived. When he came home she told him she had got her results. He asked, "How did you do sweetheart?"

She said, "I passed."

He lifted her up and he said, "Well done." Watching his reaction was very emotional. He was so proud of her, and so were Trevor and I.

It was quite an achievement for someone from a working class background to be going to university. There was a lot of excitement in our house at the time. Our friends and neighbours were so pleased for her. Audrey had said that she knew Linda would do well, but I had just hoped she would and knew that she deserved to.

Little did we know how our lives were going to change in the next couple of weeks! It was a beautiful sunny Thursday on 15 September. I kissed Dave before leaving to catch my bus for work. I can just see him now making some toast for his breakfast. Dave was on day shift. Linda had got a job where I worked, and Trevor had to go to school.

I was busy doing my work, when at about twelve o'clock there was a bit of a commotion in the messenger's room. I asked what was wrong, and one of the messengers, Jean, said there was a big fire at the place where her husband worked. We could see the smoke from our place of work. Jean finished work about an hour before me, and as she was going home, I told her not to worry, because the firemen would make sure he was safe.

When I finished work, I went straight home and really didn't think any more about it. It was always at the back of my mind how dangerous Dave's job was, but I just had to live with it. Dave had recently said that if he had his life over again, he wouldn't have joined the fire service.

I was sitting in my kitchen having a bit of lunch, when the doorbell rang. I opened the door, and there was Trevor, his headmistress and one of the firemen. Trevor brushed past me and said, "It's all right, Mum." My immediate thought was that Trevor had done something wrong.

My eyes really didn't see the fireman, Ron. He then told me that there had been an accident at a warehouse. I asked if Dave was all right, and he then said that Dave was missing. I just went to pieces. Ron said that they were doing all they could to get him out.

I knew that he wouldn't be able to survive for long, even with breathing apparatus. Only a few weeks before he had been in a fire and had to be taken out and laid on the pavement because he was having trouble breathing from being inside too long.

The news had reached Linda and she came home. We had to keep hoping, but I knew in my heart that it wasn't going to be good. Linda phoned John, who was decorating his house. He dropped everything, asked his next-door neighbour to lock up for him, and came to our house.

In the evening, the Chief Fire Officer came to the house and confirmed that Dave had died in the fire. We had reporters come to the house, and John sent them packing. They then went to our next-door neighbour's house, Mr Noakes, and he sent them on their way. He told them that he had just lost a very good neighbour and that he didn't want to talk about it to anyone.

Audrey came over to try and comfort me, but one of my bosses from work arrived and he said he thought I would be better if she went home.

Linda got some comfort from Audrey in her home. It was the worst day of my life, and I'm sure it was Linda's and Trevor's too. I don't know how we all got through it. I still relive that day every year on the anniversary.

John rang Dave's brother, Dennis, and my Uncle George. They were both shocked and very upset. One of my friends, Maureen, who lives in Banbury, Oxfordshire, was sitting in a hospital waiting room, when she read about it in the newspaper. There was a little photo of Dave. I don't know where it came from. He always avoided being pictured when he was on duty. He wasn't a showy man and never wanted to be in the limelight.

At the end of the day, John took Trevor home with him and made sure that he went to school the next day. He gave him a good breakfast before he went. He thought it would be best for him to try and get back to normal, but I'm sure that it was very difficult for him.

A short time before the accident, Dave had been at headquarters making up some ropes. He had been asked if he would do it because he was an exseaman. I think he enjoyed the time that he spent doing it. I often thought it was a shame that he wasn't still doing it at the time of the fire. I suppose that is a selfish thought, because it just would have been another poor fireman who would have lost his life.

At the time there was a flour shortage caused by a bakery workers' strike, and just before the accident I gave Dave some fruitcake to take to work which was stolen from his locker. I often wonder how the thief felt after that terrible day. I hope he felt very guilty! The next day we found out that another fireman had also died in the fire. He was a bit younger than Dave, but also married with two children.

The publicity was the worst thing for me at this time. There was something in the paper every day. I would be sitting on a bus and people would be either reading about it or talking about it. I felt that I just wanted to curl up and die. We received about a hundred memorial cards. It was nice to know that people were thinking about us, but I got upset every time that one arrived and I read it. My doctor signed me off sick from work, and the bosses were very understanding.

One of the firemen came to see me to ask if I wanted Dave to have an official Fire Service funeral. I said no, because he wouldn't have liked it. He liked to keep in the background. I went ahead and arranged the funeral for the Friday of the following week. Dave and I had never discussed if he wanted to be buried or cremated, but because of the way he had died, I didn't feel that I could have him cremated.

Because he smoked a pipe, I always said that if he died before me, I would have his pipes put in his coffin, or at least his favourite one. I asked the undertaker to do it for me. I didn't want to see him in his coffin, because I had terrible memories of seeing my granddad and my sister in theirs. Linda said that she wanted to see him, but I didn't want her to go on her own, and I said I'd have to accompany her. In the end she didn't go.

A few days after the accident, the other widow came to see me. She brought a bunch of flowers, which was really nice. It was difficult to try to console each other. I told her that Dave was such a good man; he lived for his family. He never went drinking. The only time he had a drink was if we went to some social evening; and that wasn't very often. She said that she couldn't say that about her husband, Neil. I did appreciate her visit.

The next week was an awful time for us all. There seemed to be lots of comings and goings. When the day of the funeral came, I was in a bit of a daze. The children were just as bad. John walked with the children and me from the car to the church. There were lots of pressmen taking photos outside. John stopped them from taking photos of the children and me. There was a firemen guard of honour. It was quite touching to see them, and very emotional.

I can't remember much about the service, except that Linda chose the hymns, and they were lovely. I have still got the copies that she did for me and I have often looked at them. There were a lot of people there, and I still didn't think that it was happening. I was in a completely different world. Life was never going to be the same again. It was very hard for all of us.

181

1. O God, thy soldiers' crown and guard,
   And their exceeding great reward;
   From all transgressions set us free,
   Who sang thy Martyr's victory.

2. The pleasures of the world he spurned,
   From sin's pernicious lures he turned;
   He knew their joys imbued with gall,
   And thus he reached thy heavenly hall.

3. For thee through many a woe he ran,
   In many a fight he played the man;
   For thee his blood he dared to pour,
   And thence hath joy for evermore.

4. We therefore pray thee, full of love,
   Regard us from thy throne above;
   On this thy Martyr's triumph day,
   Wash every stain of sin away.

5. O Christ, most loving King, to thee,
   With God the Father, glory be;
   Like glory, as is ever meet,
   To God the holy Paraclete.   Amen.

6th. Cent. Tr. J. M. Neale.

One of the hymns

After the funeral, we went back with the family and friends to Jim and Audrey's house. Audrey did all the catering, and felt it would be better in her house because there was more room. She did us all proud. I was grateful for such good friends.

Linda was due to go to university the week after the funeral. It was also the other fireman's funeral. I felt that I had to go because his widow had come to Dave's. It was another very emotional day and a bit like having Dave's funeral all over again. Trevor had been very quiet since his dad died; he took after his dad in that respect, never having much to say and keeping it all inside.

Linda said to me that she would stay with me and wouldn't go to university, but I knew it was important that she went. Her dad and Trevor and I were so proud of her, and Dave would have wanted her to go. I knew it was going to be hard for her, not only having just lost her dad, but also being away from home. Her birthday was coming up on 7 October, and her dad had promised to buy her a new tennis racquet, so I felt I had to buy one for her. I think John went with her to choose it.

Chapter Fifteen

The day came for Linda to go to university and John and I took her by car. It was a very long and tiring journey; all sorts of things were going through my mind. It was very hard leaving her there, and I shed a few tears after we left. I used to speak to her on the phone quite often, and a few times she said that she was going to give up, but I talked her into carrying on.

I felt that I had to get away from Reading for a few days because of all the publicity. One of the fire officers arranged for Audrey and me to go to a hotel at Eastbourne, in Sussex. Trevor went to his friend Carol's house. While we were there we went to see the convent where my sister, Frances, and I had stayed when we were younger. I had always wanted to go back, not that there were any good memories. It looked completely different because the grounds where we used to walk had been sold and built on, and the building was no longer a convent.

After that terrible day, there were collections going on in the town. Some of the money came to the other widow and me, but a lot of it was going to The Fire Brigade's Benevolent Fund. I don't think that the public were aware of this. The way that the appeal was worded gave the impression that the widows were receiving all of it.

This went on for several weeks and it was really getting to me. I saw posters around the town and in the local papers. I went to see the welfare officer at work and told her how it was upsetting me. She and one of the senior officers went to the fire brigade headquarters and asked for it to be stopped. It did make life a bit easier when this happened. I didn't object to the collections but it was so upsetting that the late firemen's names were being used.

I was off work for five weeks, and when I went back I just couldn't cope. Everyone knew what had happened in my life, and the staff had been told by a senior manager not to mention the accident. I was put on sick leave again.

Trevor was not coming straight home from school and I later found out that he was going to one of his friend's houses. He got a bit of comfort and support from her mother and the rest of the family. When I met them, I found out they were a very nice family.

I felt that I had lost all my family, what with Linda being at university, and then Trevor not coming home until late. It was very lonely. A couple of times I went for a walk by the river and wished that I had the nerve to jump in. I knew that wasn't the answer, because it would have been awful for Linda and Trevor. You don't think rationally at times like that.

The day came for the inquest. I wasn't going to attend originally, but I changed my mind and went along. It was very upsetting to hear all that was being said. There was no result and the inquest was adjourned for six months.

I had to start thinking about what I was going to do about living in a tied house. Dave and I had already talked about buying our house; in fact he had already put in a request, as his dad had left him a bit of money, which would have been enough for a deposit.

With my gratuity and the money that I had received from the public, I was able to go ahead and buy it. That gave me peace of mind. I would carry on working, which would help with the pension that I was getting. The fire brigade and the government pension was not enough to live on.

Linda had been awarded a small payment from the fire brigade to help her through university. Trevor was nearly sixteen and was thinking of doing a motor mechanic apprenticeship. He would also get a monthly payment when the time came.

I received a phone call one day from the coroner, who asked if he could call at my house to bring the death certificate. He said that he didn't want to put it in the post because of the contents. He explained that Dave had fallen through the floor and was scalded, and he wanted to know why, so he had decided to investigate. The bricks at the warehouse were made of sand and lime, and not the normal ones used in buildings, which were London bricks.

He tested them separately, by putting them in an oven, bringing them to a certain temperature, and then pouring water on them. The London brick was fine, but the sand and lime bricks just disintegrated.

He told me to go and see a solicitor, because he thought there was a case of negligence. The accident shouldn't have happened. The men shouldn't have been sent into the building because everyone had been got out and they were only trying to save a building. I did eventually go and see my solicitor, but unfortunately the coroner had passed away by then, and he was the only witness. My solicitor said that it could cost me thousands, and at the end of the day, who do you blame? I just thought that if it was brought out into the open, it might prevent other firemen from losing their lives in the future.

About six weeks after Dave died, a holiday was arranged for Trevor and me to go to Spain for a week. I wasn't very keen on going, but Trevor wanted to go. One evening we went to a social evening where a whole pig was cooked and we all sat around wooden tables and picked at it. It wasn't my scene. Trevor disappeared and when I eventually found him, I discovered he had been drinking, and felt very unwell after. It was too soon after the tragedy for me to enjoy the break.

Trevor & Veronica in Spain

I used to go to the cemetery a lot; it was only just along the road from where I lived. I would stand by the grave and cry my eyes out. Dave's death was something that I would never get over.

At the beginning people used to come and see me, but that didn't last very long. I suppose they just didn't know what to say, and I can understand that. I finally went back to work after being off for about nine weeks and after the holiday in Spain. I found it very hard speaking to people.

Linda came home for Christmas, and I hadn't done any cards, which was unusual for me. So Linda did them. She was very good at that sort of thing; she loved writing. She would always either have her head in a book or be writing.

Christmas day came and it wasn't the same without Dave, even though he might have been on duty. John came for dinner, also Mrs Ransom and Mr Weaver, who Dave used to garden for. I don't think that Mrs Ransom was very keen on him, and she let it be known.

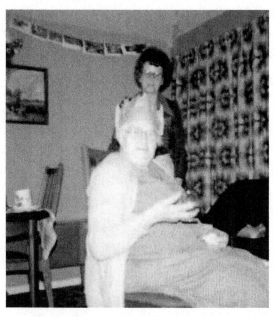

Mrs Ransom & Veronica

John asked Trevor if he would like to go to London on Boxing Day to watch Crystal Palace play, and of course he said yes. John asked me to go, but I said, "No, I'll stay at home." Anyway he persuaded me to go. We all enjoyed it and it got me away from the house for a few hours.

John came with me to the inquest, which was held in March 1978. I was a bag of nerves. The cause of death was returned as accidental. I always felt that there was something very wrong on the day of that fire, but now it was all over. After the inquest I received a phone call at work from the local press, who wanted to know how I was coping after my husband's death. It really upset me. I told one of my bosses, who asked them to leave me alone and let me get on with my life.

One of the officers came to see me to tell me that a plaque had been made in memory of Dave. He suggested that it should be put up in the bar. I said that I didn't think that was appropriate, because he didn't agree with drinking while on duty. In the end it was put up in the appliance room. I never felt that I could go and see it as it would have been too upsetting.

After doing his O Levels and GCSEs Trevor was going to leave school, as he knew he didn't want to stay on. One of the fire officers arranged for him to have some interviews for an apprenticeship. He got pipped at the post at one garage, but was accepted at another. He had to go to college one day a week. I think he found it a bit hard at first. He was still fretting about his dad and wouldn't talk about it. It was a four-year course, and I felt sure he would get his City & Guilds. He had never been academic but was good with his hands. After a few weeks he was getting a lot of skin problems, so he went to the doctor, who told him that if it didn't improve he would have to give up the job. He had been working on heavy vehicles and his hands came in contact with diesel. When the manager moved him on to cars his skin was a lot better.

Linda came home for the summer and she managed to get work again where I worked. That gave her a bit of pocket money to spend while she was at home. I went to pick her up from work one day and a letter had arrived for her so I took it with me. When she opened it and read it, she was very upset.

I asked her what was wrong and she said that Ian wanted their relationship to end. I felt really sorry for her and I thought writing a letter was a very cruel way of letting her know.

I decided to have a little break. Trevor was now sixteen and Linda nineteen, so I felt that I should be able to leave them for a while. Audrey said that she would keep an eye on them for me. My Uncle George had two chalets at Leysdown in Kent. He let me have one of those and he and my aunt stayed in the other one at the same time. I was very lucky with the weather. There isn't much in Leysdown, but I went on the beach a few times and just relaxed in general.

I had a little mishap while I was there; I was going to bed and had no shoes on my feet when I kicked a chair. In the morning my little toe was badly bruised and very swollen. I went to the hospital and after having an x-ray, was told that it wasn't broken.

When I got home, I went to see my doctor because it was still very painful and swollen. He sent me for another x-ray, which showed that it was broken. There was nothing that could be done about it, apart from strapping it to the next toe. It eventually got better, but it did take a long time. Linda and Trevor seemed to have got on all right while I was away. They were cleaning the house when I got home, and Linda cooked us a meal, which was very nice.

It suddenly occurred to me that in trying to give my children a better life than I had as a child, I had failed by not teaching them how to cook. I wanted them to enjoy their childhood. Neither of them showed any sign in wanting to learn though. I suppose all parents have some regrets when they look back. You can only do your best at the time. There is so much to do when you have to go to work as well.

Trevor got his exam results and did very well. I'm sure he could have done better, but after what he had been through with losing his dad, he did well enough.

Chapter Sixteen

After a while, John asked me out for a meal. At first I thought that it was too early, but being that I had known him for years, I couldn't see any harm in it, so I accepted. We had a nice meal and a very quiet evening. I had always been able to talk to John. After that, we went out several times, even though I felt a bit guilty.

One evening we had gone out for a drink, when John got chatting to a young woman about her dogs. She invited him to go to her place. I sat feeling very left out and a bit jealous, which surprised me as I never thought I was the jealous type. He never did take her up on her offer to visit.

When I told my Uncle George that I was seeing John, he was very pleased. He said, "Life is not to be lived on your own, darling." I must admit, it was very lonely, with Linda away at university, and Trevor was never at home. He used to encourage me to go out.

As time went on, John and I talked about getting married. When Dave was alive I had always said that if he died before me, I would never get married again. I realise now that you don't know what you will do until it happens to you. John and I had some good times together and John took me to places that I had never been before. It felt as if we were meant to be together, but I used to also feel guilty about going out with him and planning to marry him.

John & Veronica 1978

One evening we had gone out for a meal and John told me that he was going to be made redundant, as the company was folding. It was his job to shut all the shops down, so it would be a while before it happened to him. He was worried that I wouldn't want to marry him. He knew that I would be giving up my pensions if I married again. I told him I would still marry him. I knew that he would find another job; he was that kind of man. I didn't believe in living together.

I said to John one day that I thought I should let Linda and Trevor know that I was getting fond of him. He said, "Do you have to?" I decided I would.

First of all when Linda was at home, I said to her, "I am getting fond of John."

Her reply was, "That's pretty obvious."

I said, "I just thought you should know."

I then went downstairs and said the same thing to Trevor. He said, "Yeah ... Yeah..." He was waiting for me to say something else. I said, "Maybe one day I will marry him."

He was so pleased for me he threw his arms around me, saying, "Oh, Mum."

His reaction was so different to Linda's. I could tell that Linda resented my relationship with John. I found it hard to understand, because she had always thought the world of him. She was old enough to know that I had to have a life as well.

After John asked me to marry him, I said I thought we should wait until Linda finished university. He said, "Why?" I thought about it and couldn't think of a good reason for waiting. We decided to get engaged on New Year's Eve and married on 21 April 1979. At the time we hadn't realised that we had chosen the Queen's birthday, which was rather nice.

Trevor was very pleased, but Linda let it be known that she wasn't. I even considered ending my relationship with John, but then I thought why should I? Linda wouldn't be at home forever and then what about me? I did appreciate how much she missed her dad, but then so did Trevor and I. I could only hope that she would change her mind in time. I have never felt bitter towards her!

We invited Audrey and Jim to my house one evening for a drink, and to tell them our news. Audrey's response was one of disapproval. I don't think she was surprised, but didn't like what she was hearing. Jim's reaction was just the opposite. He said, "That is the best news I have heard for a long time. I am really pleased."

My Uncle George and Aunt Georgina were delighted for me, also my friends. I asked my uncle if he would give me away, and he said of course he would. John wanted to get married in a registry office, but I said that I would only get married in a church. I was brought up as a Catholic. It wasn't as if my first marriage had ended in divorce. John kept trying to talk me out of it, but

I was adamant that it was church or not at all.

We had our usual Christmas with the old folk. New Year's Eve was approaching and John asked me if I would like his mum's engagement ring or a new one. I said I would love to have his mum's ring. I think he was pleased. It's a beautiful ring. I'm sure that his mum would have been pleased.

On New Year's Eve, we invited Audrey and Jim to join us at a pub where we used to go for a meal. We had a lovely evening, and we were now officially engaged. Once we were engaged we decided to look for a property that would be ours. John had his own house and by this time I owned mine. We would buy something together. I had always wanted a bungalow; I suppose it was because of living in the prefab where Dave the children and I were so happy.

We put our houses on the market and I got a buyer almost straight away. The buyer was the son of our neighbours. John and I looked at a few places; one was a new four-bedroom house. It was very nice but because John's house wasn't selling, we got gazumped. It was rather annoying because it wasn't offered to us at the higher price it eventually went for.

We then found a bungalow that we liked and as far as we knew everything was going through. I got a phone call one afternoon from our solicitor, and he said that if we didn't sign by 4 pm that afternoon, we would lose it. I rang John, who was in London, and explained the situation. He rushed home and contacted the solicitor, who told him he was too late, even though he was back before the deadline. We were gutted. We had no idea that there was someone else trying to buy the property. It seemed very unfair.

After that, I said to John, "I think we had better start looking in a different area." We had been concentrating on Tilehurst, because we both liked it there. I looked in the local paper and saw three properties on the north side of Reading, at a place called Caversham Heights. The first one I knew I wasn't going to like before we even went inside. It was on a housing estate that didn't have a very good reputation. The second one was too pricey and the layout was not suitable.

As soon as we viewed the third one, we could see that it had some potential.

It consisted of three bedrooms (one small) and a bathroom upstairs, an L shaped lounge and dining room, a small kitchen, and a cloakroom off the hallway. The kitchen units were very dated; I think they were the originals, and the house was built in the fifties. It had a large secluded garden that was separated by a row of trees. The part of the garden nearest to house had beech hedges about eight feet tall down both sides.

John went down to the bottom of the garden on his own, and I happened to be looking out of the window when he was coming back. Seeing the look on his face, I knew it was going to be the house for us, even though it had been neglected and needed a lot of work. We went back to the estate agents and offered the full price which was accepted, and then John got on to the solicitor and told him that we didn't want to lose this house.

Chapter Seventeen

Audrey and I went to London to buy my outfit for the wedding. I found a pretty cream and coffee dress; it was like a satin under dress with a lace top. I saw a little feather arrangement to go on my head, but I couldn't make my mind up about it, so I decided to leave it. I wasn't very keen on wearing a hat, which wouldn't have looked right as the dress was so delicate.

I bought a nice suit to wear for leaving on our honeymoon, and a pair of shoes that went with both outfits. I still couldn't believe that I was doing this. After I got home, I decided to get the feather arrangement after all, so I rang and I asked them if they could send it to me and charge me for the postage. It matched my dress perfectly.

There was a lot to do to prepare for the wedding. We decided to get married in a church near Tilehurst at Theale. We had to say that we were living in the area, so friends let us use their address. It was a bit naughty but I didn't want to get married at my local church. We arranged to see the priest. We had to have several visits to talk about different things, and the priest mentioned that any children born to the marriage had to be brought up as Catholics. John wasn't very keen on that idea. He didn't like the idea of going for the talks anyway.

We booked the church for 12.30 then ordered the flowers except the ones for the church; I thought I would buy them from the market because they would be cheaper. I booked a photographer to take the pictures on the day. We decided to have the reception a few miles from the church at a cosy hotel, The George at Pangbourne. John arranged the honeymoon; all I knew was that we were going to Scotland. By this time John had been made redundant so he had plenty of time to make all the arrangements.

Leading up to the wedding day, I sensed that Linda wasn't very happy about me getting married again, and it was beginning to concern me. I even thought of calling the wedding off, right up until the day before. Linda was twenty years and six months old, and I had never objected to her boyfriends, but always made them welcome. If she had wanted to get married, I wouldn't have stood in her way. I realised it wasn't quite two years since her dad died, but I didn't choose for him to go. I will never forget that terrible day.

Trevor had a completely different attitude towards the situation. I think he just wanted me to be happy again. I would never forget Dave or the twenty happy years we shared together, many of them with the children. It wasn't always easy; money at times was short, but we managed. I always made a little go a long way and never got into debt. If we didn't have the money for something, we went without. We never had expensive holidays.

Our wedding day was approaching fast and there seemed to be a lot of things to do at the last minute. My Uncle George was coming with my aunt Georgina from Kent; he was going to give me away. John went out with his mates two nights before the wedding on a stag do. I went around to his house to do a few things, but I was given instructions not to be there when they all got back.

On the morning of the wedding I started to get cold feet, but I managed to get myself ready. It was a nice bright day, but very windy. A Rolls Royce arrived to take me to the church. I had no idea what car John had ordered, so it was a lovely surprise. I felt really good in my dress. We were a bit too early for the service so the driver took us for a ride. I found out afterwards that my elderly neighbours, Mr & Mrs Noakes, had wanted to see me in my dress. I wished they had asked me. I regret not inviting them to the wedding, but we didn't want a big do.

Mr & Mrs Noakes

The church was very modern, and I thought the service was lovely. John was dozing off to sleep; he said it was boring. After the photographs were taken, John invited some of my friends from work to join us at the hotel. We then made our way there in the wedding car as Mr & Mrs McBean. I felt like the Queen, especially as it was her birthday. The reception went off very well; everyone seemed to enjoy it. Uncle George and John's friend, Jimmy, who was best man, made a speech, and we had a few laughs. John also made his speech. I don't think anybody ever thought that John (a confirmed bachelor) would get married, but he proved them wrong.

Wedding photos

Uncle George & Veronica

John & Veronica

From left, Jimmy, Linda, John, Veronica, Trevor & Uncle George

From left, John (brother-in Law) Pamela, Claude,
Margaret, Nell, John, Veronica, Trevor, Linda,
Uncle George & Auntie Georgina

It was time for us to get changed and set off on our honeymoon. Everyone gathered around to wish us luck with the exception of Linda, even though Audrey tried hard to get her to come and wish us luck. I found that very hard to understand and felt quite hurt.

Someone had put some stones in the hubcap of the car, (I have found out since that it was Trevor). Lots of motorists kept sounding their horns when we were on the motorway. We had quite a long journey to our first hotel in Oswestry, Shropshire. I think it was much further than John realised. When we arrived, we went straight into dinner because it was getting late. I could hardly walk as my new shoes were killing me. We were congratulated by the waiter, but we never found out how he knew we had just got married.

Book Three

FLOWER ON THE PILLOW

Introduction

Book Three describes a new season in our lives, where we have some amazing holidays, and also encounter many different health issues – a real mix!

Chapter One

After being on our honeymoon for nearly two weeks, John decided that he wanted to get home in time for the general election. He had never missed voting and this time was a bit different because there was a woman in the running (Mrs Thatcher). We had had a lovely holiday and finished up on the Isle of Skye. I was secretly ready to go home. Trevor had been staying with his best mate's parents, and I was wondering how he had got on.

One night when we were on our honeymoon, I had a nightmare. I woke up sobbing. I had dreamt that Dave was still alive but an invalid, and that I had abandoned him. I can't imagine why I dreamt that, because I took my 'Till Death Us Do Part' vows very seriously. I never even agreed with divorce.

John and Veronica on honeymoon in Scotland

The journey home was six hundred miles and took us twelve hours. We were both very tired when we arrived back. John did all the driving because he liked to be in charge, and I stayed awake for the whole of the journey, which was unusual for me. We'd had a mixture of weather while we were away; some lovely sunny days also some snow.

I was now living with John in his house. Trevor was also with us. It seemed very strange. The sale of my house was completed soon after we got home. John was amazing, he did all the packing and arranging to move the contents of my house to his house. We sold a few pieces of furniture.

I still couldn't believe that I was married again. I had always thought that if anything happened to Dave, I would never re-marry, but now I realise that you don't know what you will do until it happens to you! I was still a young woman when I was widowed (just forty). I was finding it hard to adjust to my new life, but didn't know why. I loved John very much, and he was a kind and caring person, and I had known him for a long time. It must have been hard for him taking on two adult stepchildren, especially as Linda did not accept me getting married again, and Trevor was very withdrawn.

John was not at his best in the morning, and I found that hard to cope with. He was best left on his own, but it took me a while to realise it. He had been a bachelor for such a long time. His mum had been dead for eight years, so he had been able to do just what he wanted. He had been brought up in a very Victorian way. Everything had to be just right. He was very fussy about things.

The first morning I went back to work, I was thinking, "What have I done?" I know that I was comparing John with Dave, and I know that was wrong. Dave and John were complete opposites, but they each had different qualities. Dave was very quiet and inoffensive. John was very volatile; he seemed to get worked up about little things.

Chapter Two

Contracts had been exchanged on our house at Caversham, and we had been given a moving date for 24th May. John was very good at making all the arrangements and doing the packing. We were getting excited about moving into our house. It was a new beginning. John's friend Jimmy came to help us with the move. My main job was to keep the men going with food and drink.

We were a bit surprised when we arrived at the new property, because it wasn't very clean. I told John that I wouldn't put anything in the larder (food cupboard) until it had been cleaned and painted with emulsion. I ended up washing all the walls in the house. The drains outside smelled awful!

The previous owner came back to collect a boat that she had left outside. John stayed out of the way for fear of what he would say. Trevor said, "You have paid half the price of the house for the garden." He was probably right – it was a beautiful garden, but needed a lot doing to it. John really enjoyed being out there.

By this time, John had managed to get a job. It was selling consumables (nuts, bolts, terminals and some tools) to garages, warehouses and farms, from a van. I thought he picked it up very quickly, but he said it was just another area of selling; in other words, a different commodity. He didn't stay with that company for long because they were very pushy. Someone would ring up every evening to find out how many productive calls he had made. He had been his own boss for such a long time, so he was finding it hard.

He had just gone through three of the most stressful things in life: being made redundant, getting married, and moving. I had also gone through three of the most stressful things: being widowed, re-marrying, and moving.

John soon found another job doing the same thing. He was much happier with the new company. He used to have to travel up north one day a week to restock his goods. One evening when John was out, Linda and Trevor were in the lounge, when Linda said, "Why on earth did you have to marry him?"

I said, "Because I love him. I don't understand – you idolised him before."

It wasn't an easy situation for any of us.

Later on that year, John received a phone call from a person from his old company, asking him if he would close down one of the old shops in Kensington, London. He had to make an offer to clear the shop of all the fridges, freezers and fixtures. He made an offer that was accepted.

We spent the next few weekends in London. I had to drive because the car that John had from his old job had been returned. He didn't like driving my car, because it had belonged to Dave. John asked Trevor if he would like to earn some pocket money, but he said no. Our friend Jim helped for a couple of weekends and his son, Kevin, helped as well. The money we made paid for our house to be rewired. We had plans to build an extension on the back of the house. We needed a bigger kitchen and a utility room.

We had a wonderful view of our garden from the kitchen. We had all kinds of birds including the green woodpecker, which would go for the grubs in the ground. The red spotted woodpecker fed off the grubs in the willow tree. John and I had never taken much interest in birds so it was all new to us and very exciting. One day I went in the garden to hang some washing out and when I went back into the kitchen, there was a duck on the window sill trying frantically to find its way out through the window. I opened the window to let it out. I don't know who was more frightened, the duck or me! Life at our new home was very interesting. We were only two miles from Reading town, but it was open countryside at the bottom of our road.

One day from our kitchen window, I saw what looked like a dog in the garden. I just kept staring at it and then it went away. By this time we had got to know a few of the neighbours, and I was telling one of them, Doreen, what I had seen. She told me that it was probably a muntjac deer. I was quite excited to think that we had such animals in our garden, being as we were so near to the town. That wasn't the end of the wildlife in our garden; we frequently had a visit from a fox. I was getting my washing in one night and one came really close to me. What an experience! There were also badgers around but we didn't see any until years later.

Chapter Three

Linda came home from university and things were very strained. She never tried to get on with John. He went up to her bedroom one day and put his arms around her to try and have a chat, but she just pushed him away. He didn't want to take her dad's place, but did want to get on with her. John used to get annoyed because when she was at home she didn't do anything in the house to help. He said to her one day, "Your Mother goes out to work, and it wouldn't hurt you to do a bit of hoovering or ironing." She never answered him. I always felt that I was piggy in the middle. I also blamed myself for not getting her to help when she was younger. It would have helped had she got a job during her holidays, but she didn't want to.

John and I were starting to think about what we wanted done in our house. We decided before we did any decorating that we would have new doors fitted. Our friend, Jim, was a carpenter, so John asked him if he would like to earn some extra money by fitting the new doors.

We chose some teak doors and a solid front door with some little panes of glass at the top to let the light in. Jim came and hung them for us. We had a few estimates for having the house rewired and we decided on one person. John asked him if he could start as soon as possible. I left all that kind of thing to John; he was better at it than me. His past experience as a supermarket manager helped; he had been used to taking on staff.

Christmas was approaching and it was going to be our first one together as a married couple. We wanted to have a good time with Linda and Trevor. John got up early on Christmas day and lit the coal fire to make it welcoming for us all. I have always loved an open fire. We had bought presents for each other and for Linda and Trevor. What I didn't know until then was that John had bought surprise presents for both of them. He bought tools for Trevor, things that he would need in his job. Linda had a tea set called 'English Rose' so John bought her some dessert dishes. When she opened her present she said, "I'm not collecting the whole set." I couldn't believe what I was hearing. It was so very hurtful. John just wanted to give her a surprise. I thought she was so ungrateful. I really felt for him.

Linda went back to university after Christmas and we settled down again. John started to do some work on our kitchen ceiling. He had to scrape all the old distemper (paint) off which was very hard work, but John was a grafter, and he never minded doing menial tasks. In between working in the house, John would go down the garden and do some work. He knew what he wanted to do. Eventually he wanted a vegetable garden. He had had one in his old garden even though he was on his own. He enjoyed giving the vegetables away. Our garden was very secluded; it was a delight to be in it.

John asked our friend Arthur (his ex-neighbour) if he would draw up some plans for us, and he agreed. We wanted to build a new kitchen, utility room and rebuild the garage. The old kitchen was going to be a breakfast area.

During that summer Linda met up with someone called Gary whom she used to know at Red Cross. She started going out with him. Sometime later she asked me how I would feel about having him for a son-in-law? I said, "Fine." I had no objections. I really didn't know much about Gary, apart from what his job was, and that he dropped out of university because of a nervous problem. He was also in the Civil Service.

Linda had finished her three years at university. She got a good grade considering she went just after her dad had died. It must have been very difficult for her. She got the date for the graduation, but she made it quite clear that she didn't want John there. She said that she could only get two tickets and that she wanted Trevor and me to go. I told her that if John couldn't go then I wouldn't. She managed to get another ticket. John booked to stay in a hotel at Machynlleth; which was not far away from Aberystwyth. John asked Linda and Trevor if they would like to stay with us, but they said no. I'm not sure where Trevor slept that night. Linda wouldn't even join us for a meal. It was a very upsetting time for John and me; we both loved Linda very much, but we felt that we weren't needed. I don't think she realised that it was just as hard for me that her dad wasn't there. Just because I had re-married, didn't mean that I didn't experience the sadness.

Veronica, Linda and Trevor at Linda's graduation

After Linda's graduation, she went to Law School. She seemed to be enjoying it and during her time there she managed to arrange articles with a solicitor's firm. This was usually a difficult thing to do. We were very pleased for her.

When Linda was at home, we went for a walk one evening and I asked her if she thought I was having an affair with John while her dad was alive? She said, "Don't be so stupid."

I asked her, "Did you want me to be on my own for the rest of my life?" and she replied that I hadn't even tried. I said, "It wouldn't have mattered who I married, you would have been the same," and she agreed.

Chapter Four

Linda spent Christmas 1980 with Gary at his parents' house. She rang to tell me that she had got engaged. Gary had proposed to her at the place where John Constable painted 'The Haywain'. I had bought two prints after my dad died from some money that he left me, and one of them was 'The Haywain'. I told Linda that she could have it. John and I were pleased for her. When she came home, John gave her a canteen of cutlery that had belonged to his mum. It was silver-plated. He thought it would be nice because she was very fond of his mum and thought of her like a grandmother.

Sometime later Linda wrote the following article for the local paper:

That magic moment

AT Christmas time 1980 my boyfriend Gary asked me to go with him to stay with his parents in Suffolk.

Gary had often told me about his favourite place near his home and had promised that one day we would visit it. The place is Flatford Mill made famous by John Constable's painting "The Haywain", a print of which had hung on our living room wall throughout my childhood.

On Christmas Eve morning Gary told me he would take me to see the mill, and we could see if we could spot Willie Lot's cottage from the painting.

When we got to the mill I put my wellies on and we trudged along by the river.

We walked back over a bridge towards the mill. As we rounded the bend I spotted the cottage still much the same. I leaned against the white gate and watched the ducks.

Gary asked for the camera which was in its case in my pocket. He took a photo of my wellies and all and then came up to me and put his arms round me. He said: "Linda, will you marry me?" I could hardly believe it and said "Yes" and hugged him. It was such a magic moment.

Then he said: "I've got a little present for you". I thought he meant a Christmas present. But out of the camera case (which had been in my pocket all

along!!) he pulled a small blue box which he opened and put a diamond solitaire engagement ring on my finger.

I was so surprised I couldn't speak. We had talked about getting married one day but to be proposed to in such a special, beautiful place was so romantic.

When we got married last October my mum gave us the print of the Constable which hangs on our lounge wall as a constant reminder of my most romantic moment.

I might add that we are happily married and Gary is still romantic and ofen does little things which remind me that he's really the sweetest guy ever.

In February 1981 I went to work and because I was very early, decided to write a letter to Linda. I kept my portable typewriter in my desk drawer and because I found writing painful, I used to type my letters. After I had typed

185

the letter, I lifted my mug (a smoky glass one) out of the drawer to make room for the typewriter, and it slipped. As I tried to catch it, I cut my hand in between my small finger and the next one on my right hand.

Someone tried to get a clean handkerchief from one of the men, but no one had one. Eventually the first aid person took me to hospital. When I finally got to see a doctor, he said, "How on earth did you do this?" I then told him. He asked me if I could bend my finger but I couldn't. He then said, "This is going to be a difficult one. You are going to need a graft."

I didn't know what he meant, but as the nurse was going to stitch it, she said to the student nurse who was with her, "Look can you see the tendon?" Apparently I had cut the tendon. I was then taken home. It was the day that Prince Charles got engaged to Diana, 24 February 1981.

When John came home, I opened the front door and I was hiding my hand behind my back. I then told him that I had been home all day because I had had an accident. When I told him that I had cut the tendons in my little finger, the look on his face said it all. He had experienced seeing people with cut tendons. I had no idea how serious it was. I had to wait two weeks to have an operation.

When I went into hospital, I quite innocently thought that I was just going to have my finger cut (the doctors didn't tell you much in those days). A lady in the next bed asked me if I was nervous, I said "No, it's only my little finger." Little did I know! My arm was all padded up and held in a sling attached to a pole to keep it elevated. During the night I was in terrible pain and wandered around the ward until a nurse came and asked me if I was all right. I told her I needed something for the pain. She gave me some paracetamol. They were useless. The next morning when I was told that I could go home, I rang John.

He said, "I've just got to go and get some shopping at the market."

I said, "No, I want you to come and get me right now!" So he did.

I knew that I was going to have to go back into hospital to have another operation in six weeks' time, and also have some intensive physiotherapy. In the meantime I had to go back to have the stitches out. Once the bandages came off and I saw my hand, I nearly passed out. John got me onto the bed and asked the nurse to get me a glass of water. I realised why I had been in so much pain. The palm of my hand had been cut as well. They had put a rod in the palm of my hand for the tendon to grow through. I was dreading going back into hospital, because they were going to open up the same wounds again. In fact I told John that I was not going back in. He said, "You have to, because the rod has got to be taken out."

After the second operation, I decided to go to my sister Pamela's for a week. I was surprised to discover that she never got up in the mornings to see the children off to school. They asked me to call them in the mornings.

I had several months of physiotherapy and there was no improvement in my hand. The physiotherapist asked me how I got on with my doctor, I said, "I get on well with him."

She said, "I recommend that you ask to see a Mr Evans at Wexham Park Hospital, Slough. He specialises in hands." I went to see my doctor and he said that he would write for an appointment.

Linda came home for Easter and I was surprised that she didn't ask me how my hand was. When I mentioned it to her she said, "Oh I knew if I asked you, you would go on and on about it." I was very upset about her reaction and ended up in tears. When John came in, I was in our bedroom. He asked me what was wrong and was very surprised and upset when I told him.

John did some work in the bathroom. He made a hole in the wall between the bathroom and Trevor's bedroom to fit a cabinet in the recess. There was dust everywhere. I went mad! We were also going to have a new bathroom suite. I decided I wouldn't let it upset me in the future: after all it would all look nice in the end. I found it hard having the place in a mess all the time. I had always been house proud, but I learnt my lesson.

The work on our extension had started and John was helping to demolish the old outhouse when he trapped his fingers under a block of bricks that he was lifting. We had to go to the hospital and Linda had to drive because my arm was still in a sling. He had crushed the top of one finger and the end of it was numb.

It continued to be a turbulent time in our family. Linda and Gary decided that they wanted to get married in the October. It wasn't a very convenient time for us, but it was their choice. I said to Linda, "There are two things that I want to say to you, first of all, I hope you are not getting married to get away from home. The other is, don't you think it is the wrong time when you are in the middle of your law exams?" She never really answered me. She had always done so well with her studying and exams, I thought it would be a shame to fail now! She had managed to get a place at law school and articles with a solicitor.

The wedding arrangements started to take place. When Dave died, Linda told John that if she ever got married she would like him to give her away. Now the time came, she said that she didn't want that. She was going to ask someone that we didn't know. I was very upset, and said to her, it was bad enough that her dad wasn't here to do it, but now she was rejecting John. It wouldn't have been so bad if she had asked Trevor to do it. In the end she agreed to John doing it. It was very upsetting for him because he would have done anything for her.

They decided that they would like the reception at The George Hotel, Pangbourne, which is where John and I had ours. I think Gary assumed that John and I would pay for everything. He asked me what we wanted them to pay for. All they paid for were the photographs. I gave them the deposit for their flat. Things were very strained between the four of us.

I told Linda I would buy her dress and I was looking forward to taking her. She decided that she wanted Audrey to come with us. I didn't mind, but I always thought it was a Mother-Daughter thing. In the end I was glad that she came because the dress that Linda chose was not the right one for her. Audrey agreed with me on my choice. I think Linda thought it was about the cost, but it wasn't. I just wanted her to have what she looked best in.

We had to go to the church for the rehearsal and there was another issue: Gary didn't introduce the Best Man. John had to introduce himself to everyone. It was all very strange, not the happy time it should have been.

The shell of the extension was well on the way, but there was no way that it was going to be fitted out in time for the wedding. Gary arranged for us to meet his parents, and they came to our house. His mum was surprised to see how young I was (44). They seemed nice people. John asked if they would like to look at the extension, his mum said she would, but his dad wasn't interested. We didn't get to see them again until the wedding day because they lived in Ipswich, Suffolk.

Audrey and I went to London to buy my outfit. I bought a very nice grey suit and a pastel pink blouse and hat. When I got home, John loved the suit and blouse, but didn't like the hat at all. He told me to go and put it on the compost heap! I must admit that I wasn't too sure about it, but I didn't expect his reaction. I eventually went out and bought another blouse (a maroon one) and a hat to match, and John was happy with the change. I suppose I was lucky that he took such an interest in what I wore.

John and I invited my sisters to the wedding, but Gary didn't seem very happy about it. Linda invited some of her friends, so I couldn't see why my sisters couldn't be invited. In between making the arrangements for the wedding, Linda sat her final law exams. She wouldn't get the results until November. It was a very stressful time for everyone.

Three weeks before the wedding, I got up one morning to find that Linda was having terrible pains in her stomach. I asked, "Why on earth didn't you wake me up?"

She said, "I didn't like to."

I rang my boss at work to let him know that I would be late, and took her to the doctors. The doctor examined her and gave me a letter to take her to the hospital. He thought she might have appendicitis. After waiting for several hours, the doctor said he thought it was appendicitis and that they would operate later that day.

When I went to see the doctor, he said "We are not sure yet what the problem is because it could be irritable bowel syndrome." Eventually they decided to operate and she was taken to the anaesthetic room, but was sent back to the ward because of an emergency. She finally had her operation later that evening. Gary had been living in their flat, and he decided that when Linda came out of hospital that she should also stay there. John wasn't very happy about it, and I couldn't see why she couldn't come home so that I could look after her.

The day of the wedding arrived and Linda had asked Audrey to do her hair on the day. She had been practising beforehand. She took my car and drove to Audrey's house. I was beginning to get a bit anxious because the time was getting on. When she got home, she still had curlers in her hair, and I asked why. She replied, "Audrey couldn't get my hair to go the way that she wanted it. She thought it was because I took my own shampoo, which I hadn't done when she practised on me."

I had the job of brushing her hair out, and it looked lovely. It ended up in a pageboy style. She had gorgeous strawberry blonde hair. She said to me, "You are more nervous than me, Mum," but it isn't every day that you see your daughter getting married. All kinds of things go through your mind. You just want them to be happy. She looked so beautiful

John had ordered a Rolls Royce car as a surprise for her. He felt really proud to be giving her away. The weather wasn't very kind: it was raining most of the day.

The wedding and the reception went off very well and some people came back to our house after. Gary hadn't told Linda where they were going for their honeymoon. He just told her to pack her passport. They went to Guernsey. At the reception I said to Gary, "Be careful with her," meaning she might be a bit sore after the operation. He said, "I'm not driving!"

Linda and Gary's Wedding Day 10 October 1981

Linda and Trevor

Veronica

Linda and John

From left front: John Atherton, Leslie, Frances, Gary, Linda, Veronica, Pamela and Margaret. Back from left: Trevor, Claude and John

Chapter Five

At the beginning of 1982 our extension was finally finished. There were so many cupboards that I thought I wouldn't remember where I had put anything. I soon got organised. We bought some new saucepans because we had a ceramic hob. Ceramic hobs had just come on the market, and you had to have special flat bottom saucepans to use on the hob. They were very expensive, but well worth it. I am still using them now after twenty-eight years. I had never cooked with electric, so I was a bit apprehensive about it, but I needn't have worried, and I certainly wouldn't go back to gas now!

It was nice to be straight after not having a sink with running water in the kitchen for three months, even though John had rigged up something temporary in the middle of the kitchen. John fitted all the units and did all the tiling on the walls and floor; we had ceramic tiles on the floor of the kitchen and utility room. It all looked lovely. John worked very hard and did a very good job.

We decided to decorate our bedroom next, and have some new curtains and carpet fitted. There was one cupboard and two fitted wardrobes in the room. We decided to buy a little combination wardrobe-dressing table. Years later we found out that neither of us had ever liked it, so Trevor ended up having it. The window sill was very low with a brilliant view of the garden. Trevor's room had the same view, but now that the extension was finished he also had the flat roof outside his window. Having a flat roof was another thing that we regretted, because it needed a lot of maintenance.

Later on that year I was referred to the surgeon, Mr Evans at Wexham Park Hospital about my hand. He examined me and said that he thought there was something going on inside the palm. He said, "You've got three choices, one, leave it alone; two, start all over again with the operation, but

I don't think you would want that? The third choice is let me have a look inside to see what is going on." I decided to go for the third option, and he discovered a growth that had grown over the scar. After the operation, Mr Evans said, "I'm sorry that I couldn't do anything about your bent finger."

John and I got on very well although we had our ups and downs, which I found very hard at times. Usually our arguments were over silly little things. It must have been very hard for him to take on someone else's children. He had always been very fond of them, but living with them was a different thing. I always thought that John missed out on a lot during his childhood. Losing his dad when he was only five affected him badly. To me he always seemed to be insecure, but he certainly kept it hidden.

We used to go out for meals sometimes, but I was a bit of a stick in the mud! I would much rather cook a meal at home. It was nice now and again as a treat.

I had been off work for two separate six-month periods because of my accident, and the doctor wasn't keen for me to do the same job. A vacancy came up at work in the post room, and I asked the welfare officer if I could apply for it. It was an early start at seven o'clock, which suited me fine, because I had always been an early morning person. The welfare officer didn't think I should apply, but I went into work one day and I saw the senior officer who was in charge of the post room. I asked her about the job, and she said that if my doctor was happy for me to do it, then she would be pleased to give me a trial period. I was quite excited about it, because I wanted to get back to work.

I soon got into the swing of things, and I really enjoyed the job, but I found it very painful because there was a certain amount of writing to do. When I told John that I didn't think I would be able to continue, he got a bit annoyed with me, and I ended up in tears. I decided I would try to learn to write with my left hand. It was a bit hard at first but I mastered it in the end. The bank never ever questioned my signature! I realised later that John was only trying to help me come to terms with my accident, and he didn't want me to give up.

Sometimes there were mountains of post to sort out which was mostly done by morning part time staff. The full time staff had to also deal with the outgoing post. Everything had to be weighed and all the recorded and special delivery post had to be entered in a book. It was quite an interesting job, because it was a big department with initially three offices in Reading. We had to make sure that the post went to the right person or section. There were so many sections and they all dealt with different commodities. I suggested making a list of where different forms and letters went in the department, and this was recognised as an achievement when I got my annual report.

Eventually I had to see a doctor who worked for the Government. He examined me. and in his report he said that I could continue to work in the post room, so I was given the job permanently. I was very happy about the decision and when I got home and told John, he was delighted for me because he knew that I was enjoying it. Our friend, Audrey was already working in the post room, and she was a great help to me.

John was working very hard, doing his job, working on the house and doing the garden. He was a real grafter. He really loved working in the garden. It was like being in another world; it was so peaceful!

Trevor was coming up to his twenty-first birthday. Unbeknown to John, I had been saving up to buy him a portable television. John wasn't very keen at first because I had always said that I didn't want a television in the bedroom. I got my own way in the end though! On his birthday, he received a phone call from a girl that he knew called Karen, and they started going out together. I got on quite well with her. She was a hairdresser and she used to do my hair for me. I always insisted on paying her, because I thought if they split up, I wouldn't want her to be able to say to Trevor that she did my hair for nothing. John wasn't very keen on Karen and he didn't hide it.

While I was attending the hospital in Reading for my physiotherapy, I met an elderly lady called Miss Alice Appleton. She was eighty-nine, nearly ninety. She was a lovely person and lived on her own. One day I asked her how she got to the hospital, she said, "I walk." It was quite a long walk for someone of her age. I told her that if she wanted me to, that I would pick her up. I had to pass her road to get to the hospital.

She was having treatment for a whitlow on her finger. She was always complaining that the doctors messed her finger up. We became good friends, and I took her shopping when she needed to go. It would be her day, and then we would have some lunch before I took her home. I remember she always had fish and chips, but she wouldn't have the fish if it had the skin on it.

Sometimes I took her to my house and in fine weather she would sit out on the patio. John and I got to be very fond of her. Miss Alice, which is what we called her, had never been married. She and her sister were in service all their working life. Her sister was the cook and she was the housekeeper. Her sister had died about fifteen years before I met her. She missed her terribly and wasn't very good at looking after herself. She hated cooking.

If the weather was very bad, John and I would take her a meal. One day when we called, her front door was still locked. It had been snowing and was very cold. When she eventually opened the door she was still in her nightwear and she hadn't done her hair, which she usually wore in a bun. When she saw John and me standing at the door, she let us in and said, "I don't want any food!" She was trying to thread a needle and was getting rather frustrated, so I did it for her. After a while she settled down, I helped her get dressed and did her hair. She did eat the meal that we took her. John said to me later, "You can do anything with her! I don't know how you do it."

When Miss Alice was fifty she was going to get married. Everything was arranged but she couldn't go through with it. She told me that she didn't want to leave her sister. When they retired they bought a little terraced house, two up two down and a little scullery. There was no bathroom and the toilet was outside. They led a very frugal life, going without heating much of the time.

She came to stay with us at Christmas, and when she went to bed she found that we had given her a hot water bottle. She said, "Can I keep this for the night?"

I said, "Of course you can."

In the morning John took a radio up to her bedroom so that she could listen to the carols. It had to be turned up loud, because she was very deaf. It was so rewarding to watch her enjoyment in being with us. She had a marvellous appetite. I did a choice of two desserts and she had some of both.

We asked her if she would like to come on holiday with us, and she did. We were going to Cornwall, to a two-bedroom chalet . She hadn't had a holiday for thirty years. We used to go to the main building some evenings. A band was playing one evening and she made a bit of a fuss because of her hearing. We decided to go back to the chalet, and as I helped her get undressed for bed, she apologised. She realised that she had been a bit naughty. We had a good holiday, and we didn't mind that we couldn't do as much walking as we would have liked.

One day a nurse called at Miss Alice's house and discovered her lying on the floor from a fall. She was in hospital for two weeks. I went to visit a couple of times. I think the only relatives she had were two cousins, who didn't seem to bother about her very much. They decided to put her in a home. When I went to visit her she said, "This place has something to be desired." It didn't seem all that clean, but I thought the care made up for it; how wrong I was!

The home was up for sale and I was told by the new owner that she didn't want to be responsible for the way the residents had been treated, and had had them all checked by a doctor. Miss Alice had bad bedsores, and the new owner put her on a waterbed.

One Sunday John and I were going out for lunch to celebrate our wedding anniversary. After lunch, I said to John, "Can we go and see Miss Alice?", and he agreed. When we got there she was so pleased to see us. She was looking so poorly. She said to me, "I will never forget you!" That was the last time that we saw her. She died shortly after. I feel her life was cut short, and with the right care she would have gone on for a lot longer, and possibly received the Queen's telegram. Even though she was a grand age, she was very sprightly, and used to get on the bus into town on her own. I have her picture in my lounge, and will always remember her.

Veronica and Miss Alice 1984

Chapter Six

We had our friends come to stay one weekend, and were having our dinner, when Trevor and Karen came in. I wanted to get some dinner for them as there was plenty of food, but John stopped me, saying, "They told you they weren't going to be in for dinner." What we didn't know was that they had come back to do the washing up for us.

After this incident, I seriously thought about leaving John. The next morning I cleaned the house and then booked into a hotel for the night. I phoned Trevor, and my friends, Audrey and Jim, and they all came to the hotel. I went back home the next day, and things eventually got back to normal. I found it hard to accept things like that because although John was such a generous man, he would upset people quite easily.

After they had been going out for a couple of years, Trevor and Karen talked about buying a property together. Neither of them had any savings, but Trevor knew that there was some money in an account for him for a deposit on a house. Previously he had wanted to change his car, but he knew that I wasn't very keen on him having hire purchase (a form of loan). I explained that the money was for a deposit on a house when he was ready, and not for a car, so he went ahead and had the loan.

John and I went with them to view properties. They found one that they liked. It was near the town and not too far from his work. Karen never had a proper job; she used to do a bit of freelance hairdressing.

In the middle of all this, John's aunt died and left him some money. John had lived with his aunt and uncle for a long time when he was young, when his mum had to have a serious operation on her back, and they treated him like a son. They had one daughter, Margaret, and John thought of her like a sister. John gave Trevor some of the money towards his deposit. We advised

Trevor to have an agreement drawn up legally to protect his deposit, because Karen wasn't putting any money into the house, and if they split up in the future he would have some protection.

One day when I was at work, I had a phone call from Karen, asking me to meet her at lunchtime. I wondered what it was about. We met in a nearby hotel. We got a drink and I asked her why she wanted to meet.

She said, "Trevor told me that you want me to sign an agreement to protect his deposit money."

I said, "Yes that's right."

She then said, "What if I don't sign it?"

I said, "He won't get the money."

She said, "I don't understand why."

I explained, "It's as if Trevor has paid for a room in that house with his money, and if the house goes up in value, so does his room. So if things don't work out between you, he should get his deposit back, plus a percentage increase."

She finally understood what I was saying and decided to sign. Trevor had to sell his car to pay the legal fees, but one of our neighbours sold him an old car at a cheap rate.

They put an offer in on the house and the sale went through without too many problems. With our help they got some furniture together. Our insurance man gave them a freezer. We managed to buy a second hand cooker. We gave them our dining room table and chairs because we had bought another one. My ex-neighbour's son gave them some of his late mother's furniture. Linda and Gary gave them the money for a new bed. They also had a lot of small things, such as cutlery that came from Miss Alice's home.

The day came for them to move in and John and I went to help. The place had been left rather dirty and John and I started to clean up. Karen was nowhere to be seen; she was out at the shops with her mother. It wasn't a very good start! One thing that I can say about Karen is that she was a good cook. John and I were invited to dinner one day and the meal was lovely.

They hadn't been together very long, when John and I called in to see them. We picked up that things were not going very well. Trevor was in a terrible mood; I had never seen him that way before. I called in one day after work to ask Karen what was going on, she said, "We aren't getting on very well. We're always arguing." I asked her if she would like a lift as she said that she was going out. I later found out that she was going to see a solicitor.

The following weekend, I rang Trevor and asked him if he was all right and he replied he was. I sensed something was wrong so I said, "What is it?"

He replied, "Oh Mum, I've made a terrible mistake. Karen's gone."

I told him, "You haven't made a terrible mistake. It would have been a lot worse if you'd married her." Karen was also supposed to give Trevor pocket money, but didn't.

I went into the garden to tell John, who came inside and rang Trevor and told him to come up to our house straight away. When he arrived, John took Trevor's car keys and then gave him a drink to calm him down. He told us that Karen had taken his watch, a lot of the household things, and even his jumpers, leaving him feeling cold.

I phoned our solicitor to arrange an appointment for Trevor and we went with him. He couldn't see our solicitor, who was on holiday, so he had to see someone else. We were under the impression that being with someone for less than six months meant Karen would not be classed as a common law wife, but the solicitor said, "Tell me about it. There's no such law."

Karen had not put a penny towards the house and the agreement between them was that he would pay the mortgage and all the bills, with the exception of the phone bill, because she used it for work. Her name was put on the deeds because Trevor didn't earn enough money to get the mortgage on his own, and we didn't know that we could have stood as guarantors for him. Karen had used an agent who compiled some fictitious information about her earnings. She was then supposed to give him some money towards the bills, but that never happened.

Karen got it into her head that she wanted the house. When Trevor asked her how she thought she was going to pay the mortgage because she didn't have a job, she said she would get some lodgers in.

The solicitor suggested that Trevor offered her £1,000. When we got home and discussed it, I said to Trevor, "No don't offer her £1,000, offer her £800, because whatever you offer her she will ask for more." Sure enough she settled for £900. She also made a list of all the things in the house that she wanted, including the bed that his sister and brother-in-law had bought. Trevor didn't have the money, and was going to cash his endowment policy in, but we decided to lend him the money.

The day came when a friend of hers came to the house to collect everything. Poor John had the job of being in charge and I had said to him not to let her have the headboard of the bed. John also made sure that the freezer didn't work. After everything had gone, the friend came back asking for the headboard. John said, "What headboard? There wasn't one on the list!"

The mortgage society assessed his income and expenditure and agreed that he could have the mortgage in his name.

Trevor started to settle down and one of his friends moved into his house to help with the mortgage payments. About a year later when he got his statement from his insurance company about his endowment mortgage, Karen's name was still on it. The solicitor hadn't done her job properly. I took over sorting it out, and eventually got her name removed from the documents. Trevor could now get on with his life, knowing that Karen would have no entitlement to the house in the event of his death.

Chapter Seven

John and I decided to give the younger four of my sister's stepchildren a holiday. We had David and Rosslynn for a week. They had never had a holiday before, and we spoilt them, giving them a cooked breakfast every day and taking them on days out locally, and to London. John knew all the important places to show them including Buckingham Palace, Horse Guards Parade and Downing Street, where you could walk right up to No 10. We also went to Trafalgar Square, where we fed the pigeons. We all had a great time. At the end of the week we took them home and at a later date we went and collected the younger two whose names were Claudia and Jonathan.

David, Rosslyn and John

Claudia and Jonathan

One day when we were out with them, Jonathan went splashing through puddles and got soaking wet. I told him off and he went into a sulk. When we got back, he said, "I want to go home."

I said, "OK, you'd better go upstairs and pack your case." So he did.

When he came down, John said, "What shall I do now?"

I said, "Just drive around the block and he'll probably change his mind."

While they were gone Claudia told me that he was always sulking. He didn't change his mind but John brought him back anyway and he settled down. We took them back home at the end of the holiday, but we were surprised and disappointed that we never got a thank you card from my sister and husband for having them.

Once when we were in Broadstairs, John and my brother-in-law talked me into going to see my mum. She lived in Margate. I had not seen her or had any contact since Pamela got married. She didn't show any surprise at seeing me. She was living in a flat in an old mansion type property, and had a lodger called Raymond whom thought of as more of a son. I don't know the his background but he couldn't read or write, and had had an accident on his bicycle, which had left him brain damaged. He thought the world of my mum and would do anything for her.

After that meeting I saw a bit more of her. She even came to stay at our house for a holiday. We took her to Towyn in Wales, where my dad was stationed during the war. I thought she would have been quite excited to go there, but she never showed any emotion at all.

John said to me one day, "You seem to get on all right with your mum!"

I said, "I've never fallen out with her. I just didn't like the way that she carried on with the lodgers."

Mum and Veronica

John and Mum

In 1985 John and I decided we would go away to a hotel in Minehead for Christmas. Some people had a coach trip planned, and we were asked if we would like to join them. We said, "Yes please!" Although we had a lovely time, I felt guilty because Trevor would normally come to us for Christmas. He told us that he didn't mind, but that didn't make me feel any better.

Veronica on the phone to Trevor, Xmas 1985

By this time Linda and Gary had moved to Ipswich in Suffolk, and she was expecting her first baby. Things hadn't improved between us because John was still not welcome in their lives, although Linda had told me that she wanted me to be included in her children's lives.

John and I decided to have a New Year's party that year. We invited some of our neighbours and we had a great time even though it was hard work. When the pub closed, Trevor turned up with some of his mates. We let two of our neighbours' children, James and Wendy sleep at our house for the night. We supplied them with goodies, and they had their own little party in their room. Those New Year parties continued every year for quite a long time.

One year Trevor said, "You aren't going to like what I'm going to say, Mum."

I asked why, and he replied, "I loved my dad very much, but in a way I love John more. He's been with me while I have been growing up."

I wasn't upset, because John had always been there for him and he knew that he would always give him the support that he needed.

The spread New Year 1985/86

John and Veronica New Year 1985/86

Trevor, Chris and Veronica New Year 1988/89

Chapter Eight

On 21 April 1986, John and I were about to go out with our friends for a meal to celebrate our wedding anniversary, when we got a phone call from Linda saying she had just given birth to a little girl and named her Rebecca. I was very excited and John was pleased, but felt excluded from the celebrations.

I arranged to go with Trevor to visit them the following weekend. As much as I wanted to see Rebecca, I was torn between going and staying with John. He wasn't very happy about me going, and I think he was also concerned about me driving all that way, as I hadn't done much long distance driving since I married him.

Rebecca was beautiful. She reminded me of Linda when she was born, except Linda was a lot smaller. It was a lovely feeling to be a grandmother, but the feeling was spoilt with the situation with John. I felt that when I was with Linda and Gary I couldn't speak about John, and when I got home I couldn't speak about Linda and Gary. I couldn't think of how I could resolve the situation.

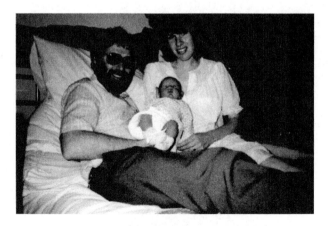

Gary, Rebecca and Linda 21 April 1986

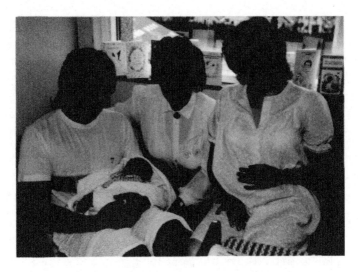

Trevor, Rebecca, Veronica and Linda

The christening was arranged for Sunday 1 June, and I spent a few days at Linda's to help with the preparations. Trevor and his friend Chris came for the day. Trevor was on crutches after having an operation on his knee. Everything went well and it was a nice day. Gary's family were there and Linda's best friend.

Linda, Trevor,
Veronica and Rebecca
The Christening

Linda, Gary and Rebecca

At around this time, John went into business on his own. He used to do a lot of thinking when he was in the bath. I went into the bathroom one day when he was in the bath, and I could see that something was on his mind but when I asked him about it, he said, "Nothing."

Later he told me that he was thinking of going into business on his own, and I immediately replied, "Well, do it!"

He explained his concerns, saying, "I'll have to take out a loan, and it means giving the bank our deeds to the house."

I said, "If it doesn't work out, we'll just have to move to something a bit cheaper," so with my support he did it, and never looked back. We went through the bad times of the eighties, but he managed to keep his head above water. He didn't make a fortune, but he was his own boss, and he was happy.

The following year I was going to be fifty. John asked me if there was anything special I would like to do, but I didn't have anything in mind. He said we would go out for a meal to the place where we went a lot before we got married. On the way there he was taking a different route, and I suspected something was going on. He had arranged with Trevor and some of our friends to go to an Italian restaurant. We had a nice evening and the owners made a cake for me.

I wanted to visit Linda and Gary and to see how Rebecca was getting on, but I didn't want to ask outright in case the answer was no, so I let it be known that I had some holiday booked in August. As I hoped, Linda suggested I visit and I always wondered if my friend Audrey had said something, as she knew I wanted to go.

It was a good week, and I was able to spend time with Rebecca, taking her out to give Linda a bit of time on her own. On the Thursday, Gary had a day off work and we went to the Suffolk Show. I enjoyed the week, but I never really felt at ease there.

Veronica and Rebecca 1987

Veronica and Rebecca 1987

In October, John and I went away for the weekend to Seaford, Sussex, near Brighton, staying in a chalet. We visited the 'Lanes' in Brighton and enjoyed looking at the antiques.

The following week was when we had the great storm. I went to work in the morning and saw all the trees that had come down, and broken branches everywhere. At one point I had to drive on the pavement. When I got to work, I rang John and told him to be careful. He said, "All right," and was a bit dismissive, as he had slept through the storm, but he got a rude awakening when he went out.

When he got home after work, the first thing he did was to walk down to the bottom of our garden. Two trees from the next garden had blown down and fallen into ours. The lady who lived there had come over into our garden, wanting to cut the trees for logs. John was not very pleased, and told her so, thinking that she should have asked permission first.

For a long time I had been aware of how uncomfortable my hand was. My finger was bent over and got in the way. I decided to have part of my finger removed, and John and I went to see Mr Evans, the surgeon, privately, who agreed with me and recommended that I have the fiscal part of my finger removed.

I had the operation at St Margaret's Hospital, Windsor on 6 November 1987 under local anaesthetic. When I returned after a few weeks for a check-up, it was a bit weird seeing what was left of my finger after the dressing was removed. It took a while to get used to it, but it was much easier now, and I was able to shake hands again. I have never regretted having it done.

Christmas was coming and Trevor and I decided to visit Linda, Gary and Rebecca. John and I had bought a few little gifts for Rebecca, but her main gift was savings certificates, because we both felt that she would benefit later in life. We bought gifts for Linda and Gary, but Linda was now pregnant with her second child, so we thought it would be better to give her a cheque.

When it came to writing on Rebecca's certificates, John asked, "What should I put on these? I don't like putting John; I don't think she should call me John, as I'm her step-granddad." He decided to put, 'To Rebecca from Gran & John (step-granddad)'. I didn't think any more about it, because after all that is what he was, except he had never been allowed to be one.

Trevor and I went to visit as planned. He drove because it wasn't long after my operation on my little finger. During the night I heard Rebecca crying for a long time. I didn't want to interfere but eventually I got out of bed and found that Linda was up, but she wasn't allowed to pick Rebecca up, because she was pregnant. I thought Gary was being over cautious as she was only five months' pregnant. But I bit my tongue, and returned to bed without a word.

The next day Linda cooked a meal before Trevor and I went home. Gary poured wine for himself and Linda but didn't offer Trevor or me any. Trevor wouldn't have had any because he was driving. When we got in the car to go home I said to Trevor, "I can't believe that Linda or Gary never asked how my hand was."

Trevor replied, "I know Mum."

On New Year's Eve, John and I were preparing for our party, which took up most of the day. We received a letter in the post from Linda and Gary, saying how upset Linda was that John had signed himself step-granddad on Rebecca's certificates. They said that in future they wouldn't accept any gifts or cards with John's name. We were both very upset and I ended up in bed with a migraine. It spoilt our evening. We didn't put our friends off, but I wasn't feeling very good. The following day I rang Linda and said that I wanted to visit to discuss the blackmailing letter. Linda called Gary to the phone, who said that Linda missed her dad a lot at that time of year. We all did. Trevor and I missed him; he was a big part of our lives and would never be forgotten, but we had to get on with life.

I said, "It was funny that Linda accepted the cheque that we gave her."

He replied, "That was signed by you."

I said, "No it wasn't. It was a cheque from our joint account and John signed it!"

I said, "John would love to see Rebecca, but you won't let him, will you?"

He replied, "Certainly not."

John said that I had to do what they asked, but I never felt happy about it. It was like choosing between my husband and my daughter. It had made my life very difficult. I had never thought that I would be in the same position with Linda that I had been with my mother, but for different reasons!

I received a letter from Linda at the beginning of January 1988, and there was no reference to the previous letter. Any letters or cards were only addressed to me; there was never any mention of John. I had been very badly hurt and chose not to reply to her letter.

One day I decided to ring Linda to see how she was. When she answered the phone she was very abrupt with me, and I said, "If your dad knew how you were treating me, he would be very upset."

She said, "That's where all this started."

I replied, "It's only because you were in love with John yourself."

She said, "Get stuffed!" and put the phone down.

Her reaction confirmed my feelings. I had always thought that this was the reason she was so nasty to John. Several of my friends had said the same, because she thought the world of him before we married. We did receive a card when Hannah was born, and I sent some clothes for her. I would get quite upset at looking at the baby clothes, so John told me to buy some and send them, but it wasn't the happy time that it should have been.

John and I got on with our lives the best we could.

Chapter Nine

About this time, Trevor had another girlfriend, Amanda, who lived in Oldham, Lancashire. He brought her to meet us and John and I thought she was very nice. She was smartly dressed and worked in a travel agency. I heard that Trevor had said, "This is the one!" He used to travel up to see her some weekends.

John and I were so pleased that he had found someone that he was happy to be with. They were planning a holiday in Barbados, which I think Trevor was paying for out of his endowment money. I would do his washing for him whenever he went away, and when I saw him before he left, I said, "I bet you are really excited about this holiday."

He replied, "Not really, I wish I wasn't going."

That was a bit of a shock for John and me. Trevor is a man of few words and if he wanted us to know why he felt like that, he would tell us. A lot of the time he would speak to John.

On his return, I asked him if he had had a good holiday, he said, "Not really." Apparently, things had gone wrong a few days before they went away, as Amanda had met someone else. When they arrived back, Amanda asked him if he wanted to stay at her house overnight, but he refused and he slept at the railway station before catching the morning train home. We felt really sorry for him, but there was nothing that we could do about it; he had to work things out for himself.

Trevor is hanging his washing out in our garden. (A rare sight)

John, Trevor and I went to visit Uncle George and Aunt Georgina on the Isle of Sheppey. We had a great day with them. I took the food to make it a bit easier for them. Uncle was always great fun. He would sing and Auntie would play the piano.

John, Veronica & Uncle George 1987

Uncle George & Trevor 1987

My niece Rosslynn came to stay one weekend. She was such a helpful girl. She would do the washing up, or get the washing off the line without being asked. She's always very bubbly, and has always been my favourite. She rings quite often to see if I am all right.

Rosslynn & Veronica 1988

That year we decided to go away again for Christmas, and went to the Dudley Hotel in Brighton, Sussex. We were shown to our room and were not very impressed. The drawers were not clean and there was water coming down from the room above. John complained and eventually we were given another room. We expected a better standard because it was a four star hotel. We met Joan and Bertie there. They weren't married, but were good friends who used to go out socially together. We kept in touch with them after that.

When Bertie was coming up to his eightieth birthday, he invited us for a meal at a very select hotel in Brighton called The Grand. We had to book into a hotel for the night, because it was too far for us to go home. The evening was a bit of a disaster – the service was appalling. When we got home, I wrote and complain on Bertie's behalf, explaining that my uncle's evening had been spoilt, and listing the problems. I didn't tell Bertie that I had written until I received a reply apologising and offering a free meal including wine. I then rang Bertie, who was delighted. John and I had to book into a hotel again, but it was all well worth it. The evening was perfect and the staff were on the ball. Sadly Joan and Bertie have both since passed away.

John & Veronica Xmas 1988

Veronica, Bertie & Joan Xmas 1988

At work I was going to a promotions board. It was my third attempt, as nerves let me down on my first two. Just before I went in I saw a member of staff who had been on the previous panels and asked what I had done wrong. He assured me that I hadn't done anything wrong, and it would be alright.

As the interview began, I could actually hear my heart thumping, I was so nervous, even though I felt I was answering the questions well. I was pleased that I'd a quick look at the paper that morning, because I had to quote something that I had read. I chose an article about an insurance company that wouldn't insure people who had been prosecuted for drink driving, which is something I feel strongly about. I also read that it was going to be illegal to sell ivory, but I have since found out that this ruling applied from 1947.

The following week I saw my line manager when I was out at lunchtime, who said, "The results will be out tomorrow!" That was all she would say, but it was obvious that she knew the results, because she was grinning. I received my letter the next day, and I had got through at last. John and Trevor were so pleased for me.

Because I was the most senior person (in terms of years at the establishment) who had passed the board, I got first choice of where I would go. There were two vacancies: one was with the fraud department, and the other was at a small computer section where all the schemes were managed. It would be my job to register the users on to the system giving them access to different schemes, and be responsible for security, making sure that they were deregistered when they left.

There were only three staff; if I got the job I would be the fourth. Two members of staff would be a grade above me and one above them. I decided to go for an interview for the computer job, because the one at the fraud section involved a lot of writing and I thought I might be a bit slow because of my hand.

I went for an interview with the senior officer, Mr Rawson, who explained all about what was done at the section. I must admit it was a lot to take in at the beginning, and I had never used a proper computer, only a word processor. Mr Rawson said he would be pleased to have me join the team. I was still only part time and doing twenty-five hours a week. My hours in the post room were from seven until twelve, and Mr Rawson said that he was happy for me to continue with those hours. I couldn't have been more pleased.

My first day arrived and it was a bit daunting. I was faced with a large pile of filing; none had ever been done since the section was started up. The two managers who I worked with had no idea of the filing system. It wasn't a simple alphabetical order. I was thrown in at the deep end, but once I got stuck into it, the pile soon went down.

I had to devise my own system for getting staff registered on the system. Forms had to be filled in and signed by the administrator, but once they were sent to computer services to be added to the system, there was no record of what you were waiting for to come back. I did a minute (letter) on the computer to be sent with the application and I kept a copy so that I knew what was outstanding, otherwise there was no way of chasing things up if someone made enquiries about their registration. There had never been any kind of system set up before I arrived.

I was responsible for security; therefore I had to be aware of any of the staff who were leaving so I could have them removed from the system. Also sometimes staff moved to another department and no longer needed access. I was really enjoying my job, and nobody bothered me.

After I had been at my new job for a while, I went to Mr Rawson and asked him if he had anything else that I could do? I didn't feel that I had enough work, and had been used to being very busy. He said, "I'm sorry about that," but he didn't find me anything else to do. I offered to do some photocopying for another section, so that helped.

It was coming up to Easter and I wanted to send a little something to Rebecca and Hannah. It was also Hannah's first birthday. I bought two Easter cards, a birthday card, and three postal orders and sent them in time for Easter and Hannah's birthday. When I arrived home from work on Maundy Thursday, the three envelopes were on the doormat, returned unopened. I felt this was the last straw. I was finished with them now. I had tried to keep things going, but it was just too difficult!

I had been putting some money in a post office savings account for Rebecca and Hannah, and decided after this to close the accounts, as I couldn't see the point. I told John I would leave them some money in my will instead.

Linda and Gary went on to have two more children, but I only found out about this through my aunt. I sent Linda a birthday card for three or four years, but I never had any response, so I gave up.

Chapter Ten

John and I were sitting on our patio after just having our evening meal, and realised that our little friend the deer was in the garden. We kept very quiet and enjoyed watching him. However, later that evening when John was going down to his vegetable garden, and I took him a cup of tea after an hour or so, he said, "Do you want the bad news?"

I said, "What, has the deer eaten all the lettuce?"

The answer was, "No, but he has eaten lots of our runner beans."

There wasn't much we could do about that. We have to pay for our pleasures in life!

A very kind colleague in my office gave us some more bean plants. A few days later, at 6.45 in the morning, we had a visit from two deer, a male and a female. They stayed in our garden for nearly an hour, this time sitting down and making themselves comfortable. Later that morning we discovered that a few more beans had been nibbled. We even saw them eating the roses, but did nothing to stop them. We just accepted that they were part of the family and needed to be fed.

Because John's dad had died when he was fifty, he had got it in his head that he wouldn't get past that age. Sometime before he had told our friend Audrey that if he reached fifty he would take her out for a meal. The time was fast approaching, so John booked us all into a hotel in the New Forest for a weekend. John and I had been to the hotel before. Audrey and Jim were surprised about the weekend, and we all enjoyed ourselves.

I had already booked a surprise get together for John's fiftieth birthday with some of our friends at the hotel where we had our wedding reception, and I had arranged for a taxi to pick us up. A few days before, I rang the taxi man to check about the booking, and it was a good job I did because he had forgotten. He was one of John's customers, and I don't think he would have lived that one down if he hadn't turned up. It turned out to be a great evening. Most people came back to our house and John said it was the best night of his life. Dave, the taxi driver thanked us for inviting him into our home.

Veronica and John, June 1990

Audrey and Jim, June 1990

Later that year we were going on holiday to Scotland. We were at my sister Pamela's house, when we asked one of her stepchildren, Claudia, if she would like to come with us. She said, "Yes please." When she arrived at our house we found that she didn't have any suitable shoes for walking, or any dresses for the evenings. We were touring, but staying in hotels. On the first day, we had to buy a new hairdryer as mine had stopped working, and we also bought Claudia some shoes. When we went to Edinburgh, I took her into a dress shop and she tried on two dresses, a black one and a red one. She looked gorgeous in them both. She said, "Auntie, I can't make my mind up which one to have!" So John and I said she could have them both. She looked like a model in them. She has dark skin, so the red one looked great on her, and I believe that sometime after she got home, she did model in that one.

One day we were walking around a cemetery looking at the old grave stones as John and I liked to do that sort of thing. I saw some rabbit holes and said to John, "Be careful, there are some rabbit holes over there." The next thing, my foot had gone down one. John had to carry me back to the car and then take me to the hospital in Edinburgh where I found I had sprained my ankle badly. The next day, I was confined to the hotel while John took Claudia out, and on their return, John gave me some stickpins that he had bought for me, because I collect them. I was pleasantly surprised.

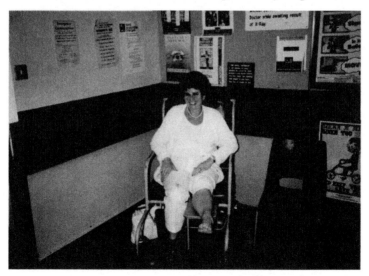

Veronica Edinburgh Infirmary 1990

Claudia Scotland 1990

Veronica and Claudia Holy Island 1990

We had a lovely holiday and Claudia had her own room in every hotel; she had never had that before. She drew a lot of attention, as at that time it was unusual to see someone with dark skin in that part of the country.

Chapter Eleven

It was 1991, and John and I went to Chester for Easter. When we arrived we decided to go for a walk but I couldn't get my walking boots on. By the next morning I had a job to walk; my legs were so swollen. We went into Chester, but I was in so much pain we decided to go back to the hotel, and we cut the holiday short and went home.

When we arrived home, John rang Trevor and asked him if he wanted to come for dinner the next day, and that he would be doing the cooking because I was having problems with my legs. When he came the next day, he was shocked to see that I had difficulty even getting to the toilet.

After Easter I went to the doctors and at first she thought that I had rheumatoid arthritis, but after seeing a specialist, I was diagnosed with a condition called fibromyalgia, and told there was no treatment or cure. Eventually I was told it was because I had had such a lot of trauma in my life, and that I had not had any counselling. The specialist said that he could still send me for counselling, but I said I couldn't see the point, because I still had the problem with my daughter and that wasn't going to change.

In June, John and I left home just before 5 am on a Friday morning to go on holiday to Northumbria. It is a very nice time of day to travel, as the roads are traffic free. I find it a delight to see all the wild life. I had counted up to twenty rabbits, when we saw at least ten or maybe fifteen all together. John slowed down so that I could see them; they were dashing to and fro. I was very excited; just like a big kid! We had just picked up speed a few miles along the road when I saw a deer out of the corner of my eye to the right. John saw it at the same time, and made an emergency stop, but still hit the deer.

John said to me, "You stay in the car while I go back to check the deer." It was dead. We were both very shaken up. In a way I was pleased that we had killed the deer, as it would have been worse to have just injured it. I asked John if there had been any damage to our car, and he replied, "You could say that." I got out of the car to have a look. The offside wing and headlight plus the front skirt were damaged, but we were able to continue our journey. Needless to say it took the shine of the start to our holiday. We realised that we had to report the incident to the police, but thought that we would wait until we reached the hotel.

We stopped in Leeds Selby for breakfast and to have a break from the driving; John always liked to do the driving when we went away, so I never took over to give him a rest. We went a bit further and decided to stopped at a place called Richmond, in Yorkshire. John had read that it was a nice town. We had a walk around looking in the antique shops; we bought a couple of small items there. We had a coffee in some nice tearooms, and then decided to continue our journey. We thought that Richmond was a very pretty place.

We arrived at The Post House Hotel, Washington, just after 1 pm. This was to be our base for the following week, so that we could tour the Northumbrian coast. We found the staff at the hotel very pleasant indeed! In fact, I would go as far as to say that they the best that we had ever experienced.

When we settled into our room, John rang the police in Reading about the deer. He was transferred to two other police stations and nobody seemed to know what the procedure was. Eventually he rang the police in Washington and was told to report in person to the police station taking his licence with him. He asked if he could leave it until the morning, because he had done a lot of driving that day, but the policeman said no.

When we arrived at the police station, John told a WPC that he had killed a deer. She looked at him as if he was mad. Then she went away to have a word with someone else. When she came back, she took John's name and address, the place and time of the incident, but I never saw her write anything down about the deer at all. It was all written on a piece of scrap paper. Then she said, "That's it then."

John said, "Don't you want to see my driving licence?"

She replied, "Not particularly."

It makes you wonder why we had to report it in the first place! Things have changed since then and you don't have to report if you hit a deer or a dog any more.

On Friday afternoon we decided to go out for a couple of hours, but as we didn't want to go too far after a long journey, we went to the Metro centre at Gateshead. We have never seen anything like it! There are so many shops that you couldn't possibly see it all in one day. It was spotlessly clean and a pleasure to walk around. Everything was there under one roof, with Marks and Spencer store and several other stores nearby.

On Saturday we went to a place called Banburgh, which was about fifty miles away. There is a Castle there, and it is the place where Grace Darling was born. Grace Darling is famous for having rescued several shipwrecked people from the sea in 1838. We went into the museum where there were several letters from the time that it happened. I found it a very interesting place. We also went into the Castle. We had some lunch at Banburgh and then moved on to a place called Seahouses as we had been told that it was very nice. We were not very impressed; it was too commercialised for our liking and not very clean.

The next day we went to the Quayside market in Newcastle. There were about three hundred stalls there; quite a lot of the things were repetitive but they were very cheap. I bought a cardigan, but that was all. It was an experience! I also wanted to see what Newcastle was like, as part of the department that I worked for had moved there.

We went on to Whitley Bay parked the car, and walked along the front to Teignmouth. We had some of the famous northern fish and chips for lunch; they were delicious! We went to a car boot sale that was along the seafront, but it started to rain; it didn't last long though. We went to a large antique market that was being held in a hotel. We bought a couple of Welsh brass lady bells, a tie pin and a hat pin, all of which I collect.

From there we took a ride around the coast making our way back to our hotel, via the Tyne tunnel. We thought that it would be an experience, as neither of us had been through it before. Once back at the hotel we had a nice bath and changed for dinner. The food was excellent!

On Monday we set off for Barnard Castle. We had a look around the town, which was quite interesting. We then went to Bowes museum where we spent a good two hours or so. John and Josephine Bowes founded the museum. Josephine was a Parisian actress. The majority of the items in the collection are French, but there are paintings from Italy and the Netherlands. John and I found it interesting but very tiring. There was a solid silver antique swan that played a tune and catches fish. There was a demonstration once a day, I think it was at midday.

We had some lunch in the museum restaurant and then moved on to a scenic route to High Falls, which is the highest waterfall in Britain (so they say!) It is 70 ft high. It was spectacular. Unfortunately by this time, the rain had arrived, so it would have been much better on a bright day. I took some pictures of the falls. We left there and drove back to our hotel via the picturesque Yorkshire Dales. Back at the hotel we had a bath and got changed for yet another superb meal.

Our destination the next day was to Hexham, a little market town. We had found out before that it was market day but we didn't think much of the market; it was nearly as bad as the one in Reading, where we lived at the time. There were quite a lot of antique shops, so because it was raining once again, we had a browse around them. We had some lunch and then moved on to Kielder Water Lake.

This is the largest man-made lake in Britain. By this time it was raining very heavily, which spoilt the view across the lake. There were facilities for various water sports, i.e. water-skiing, sailing and windsurfing. You could also hire canoes and go for boat rides. There was a forest drive around the lake that was twelve miles long. We decided to go on this drive which was very pleasant, but once again it would have been much more enjoyable had the weather been fine. Once we had driven through the forest, we made our way back to the hotel. This had been the wettest day so far.

On the Wednesday, we thought that we should see what was at Washington, as that was where we were staying. It was another covered shopping area; everything that one could want under one roof. We left Washington and made our way to Amble, which is on the north east coast. On our way home from our day out on Saturday, we had passed through a place called Warkworth, which looked a very pretty village. This was very near to Amble, so we decided to go there first. We parked the car and had a walk around. There was an old castle ruin near the river. We had a walk along the river; we took a few pictures and then went and had some lunch. After lunch, we decided to have a walk along the beach towards Amble.

It was a lovely walk that took us about two and a half hours, walking back by the river. (I wish that I could do that now!) When we got back to the village, we had tea in a place called Courtyard Tea Rooms, which was a room at the back of a gift shop. There was a courtyard where you could sit and have your tea providing that the weather permitted! The people were so friendly and everything was so clean. The weather had been better than the previous day, with only a couple of showers until 5.30 pm when the heavens opened up. We were very impressed with Warkworth.

The next day was to be the last day of our holiday. We always find that we are glad to get home for a rest; but we like to see as much of the area as possible when we are on holiday. On the final day of our holiday we went to a place called Seaham. There isn't much there, but we had a walk on the beach. I collected some very pretty pieces of glass. I even had John helping me. I ended up putting them in a glass jar. I have still got them to remind me of that holiday. We arrived back home safely on the Friday. This had not been one of our favourite holidays, but some of the places we enjoyed very much. I think we had been spoilt by going to Scotland, and there is no comparison with the scenery!

Veronica Orsborn

Banburgh Castle 1991

Chapter Twelve

That year I had planned another birthday surprise for John – a day trip on The Orient Express. Trevor joined us.

I booked the tickets and arranged the train journey over the phone. All I had to do was show my credit card when we arrived at the station. John was thrilled to bits. The day was spoilt a bit, because on the way home, I realised that I had left my handbag in the taxi. Trevor rushed back to see if he could find it, but to no avail. John had already asked me if I had everything and I said, "Don't treat me like a child!" The only important thing in my bag was my credit card, so I got that stopped when I got home.

Veronica & Trevor Orient Express

Veronica & John

One day, I saw an advert in the paper for free English tuition at one of the local schools. It was for any part of English that you needed. At that time I was still only working part time, and as I had always had a problem with my full stops and commas, I thought I would go along to find out what it was all about. I met the tutor, Jenny, who was very helpful so I decided to go to the class. I found the classes useful and I got to meet other people. We were asked to do different things, and I began to feel more confident. Jenny never made you feel inadequate.

After a few months, Jenny suggested that I sit for a City & Guilds qualification. I agreed to do it, but felt a bit nervous, especially as by this time I had a different tutor. The day came and I found it a bit daunting, because apart from taking the driving test I had never done any exams. When the results came out, the tutor rang me at home to tell me that I had failed. She couldn't believe it and told me that I was the best student in the class. A couple of weeks after, the senior tutor rang me at home and suggested that I do a GCSE in English. I said that I didn't think I was capable, but she didn't agree.

I had just decided to increase my hours at work to full time. It meant going to college once a week in the evening. When I told John he said, "You're taking on a lot, what with working full time, but if that's what you want to do, I'll help you all I can." I did find it a bit tiring, but I don't give up easily, though I did get frustrated surrounded by youngsters, who sat with their headphones on listening to music or football commentary. When I found out that I had to do Shakespeare, I thought that would be the end for me, but I continued and in the end did quite well.

The day came for my English exam. The doctor had given me a letter explaining that because of my arthritis I was a bit slower with my writing, so I was allowed a bit more time. Walking into a room full of young people was daunting. When the results arrived I was very nervous about opening the envelope, but discovered I had achieved a C grade, which I was pleased about. I hadn't told anyone that I was doing it with the exception of John and my bosses at work. Everyone was pleased for me. Trevor said, "I had no idea, Mum." A few weeks before on one of my college evenings I had asked Trevor to come and sit with John because he wasn't very well. I told him that I was doing a course for work (a little white lie).

Now that I had finished at college, I decided to learn to swim. I had never had the opportunity to learn before. I found out that our friend, Brenda, had been going to a school near her, so I decided to give it a try. I soon learnt and got my five metre certificate, and a few months later my ten metre.

Two years before my mother's eightieth birthday, I spoke to my sisters about a surprise birthday party, suggesting that we each save two pounds a week and that would give us around four hundred pounds. I said that I didn't mind opening an account to put the money in, but they didn't want to do that, so we each saved the money ourselves. I booked a hotel in Broadstairs, near where my sisters lived. The manager arranged the disco and the food. I made the cake in the shape of eighty and my colleague at work iced it for me.

From left: Pamela, Mum, Veronica & Tony

80th Birthday cake

The day came, we all had a good time but my mum got to find out beforehand as Pamela told her. I was a bit upset about that. Also, Margaret decided to go on holiday, even though the date had been arranged for such a long time. I asked Pamela and Frances about tipping the staff and the disco man, but they didn't want to, so I made my own decision and gave a tip as I believe in rewarding for good service. I was managing the money and was still able to give some back to them.

This year Bill and Sonia (our neighbours) did the New Year's Eve party, as I said to John that I couldn't do it anymore and I felt it was time for someone else to do it. It wasn't as lively as in our house, and there wasn't much music or dancing. The following year another neighbour did it, but it was a bit of a flop. After that it died a natural death. We did miss the good times though.

The year after my mum was eighty, my Uncle George was also eighty. I made him a cake with a horse on it. I rang my Aunt Georgina to ask if John, Trevor and I could visit on the day, as a surprise for Uncle George. I prepared a meal to take with us. Just before we got there we stopped and put a 'Happy Birthday' strip on the car and some balloons. When we arrived, Uncle was so shocked; he just stood and stared at us. We had a great day; plenty of laughs and singing, with my Aunt playing the piano.

Aunt Georgina & Uncle George

80ᵗʰ Birthday cake

From left: John, Trevor, Uncle George & Aunt Georgina

Uncle cutting his cake

John's birthday surprise that year was tickets to a Shirley Bassey concert at Cardiff Castle. He was thrilled and the show was fantastic.

Around that time we were thinking of changing our car and went for a test drive in a Hyundai. We then decided to go up market and get a more expensive model, and I wanted to try an automatic. The salesman let us trial the car for a whole day, and we were smitten. It had lots of extras, including air conditioning, which was not common then. We never regretted buying it.

John and I worked so well together. He always had bookwork to do in the evenings, and sometimes he would come downstairs to get me a drink. He knew that I didn't like him working so late, and was trying to keep me happy, but I also knew he had to keep on top of his bookwork. Sometimes when I opened my lunch box at work, I would find some money and a note telling me to buy a frock! It made me smile and was always a surprise. On a Saturday morning I would go swimming at the local hotel, and John would do the shopping. After I would go home and do some of the housework. When he came in I would cook him a late breakfast. He always put the shopping away, as well as making the list before he went shopping.

When our bathroom was upgraded, John fitted a cabinet to the wall. One day Trevor accidentally let the door go back on the tiles and it smashed the glass. It was bevelled glass and very expensive to replace. A few months later John and I were in the lounge when we heard a bang, and then the front door slammed after Trevor had made a quick exit. He had done the same thing again and couldn't face us. John got it repaired and he put some cord on the doors so that they couldn't hit the tiles. I can laugh at it now, but it wasn't funny at the time.

Chapter Thirteen

In May 1993 I was at home doing John's statements on the computer. It was a bank holiday. One of my mum's lodgers rang to say that my mum had been taken into hospital. I immediately rang the hospital and asked the nurse if she thought that I should come. She said, "I think that would be a good idea."

By this time John had come in. I closed the computer down and started to pack a few things, because I didn't know how long I was going to be away. At that time I had a portable typewriter, and I took that too. The traffic was terrible. It was late in the afternoon and of course the traffic was worse because it was a bank holiday.

When we arrived at the hospital, I told the nurse that I had come to see Mrs Saunders, my mum. She asked me to wait a while. We had been waiting for quite a long time, so John said, "I'm going to see what's going on! Just as he was speaking, the sister appeared and told us Mum had already been taken to the mortuary!

I was very shocked and said, "I didn't even know my mum was dead!" She wasn't aware that my mum had more than one daughter, so assumed that I knew. She took me into her office and got me a drink. A nurse brought the bits of jewellery that she had when she was admitted.

We left the hospital to go to my mum's house. Mum had given John the key to her house, but he wouldn't use it, so we rang the bell and Tony, one of the lodgers answered the door. We walked into the front room, and saw my sister, Margaret and her husband, John, going through my mum's handbag. I said, "What on earth is going on here? Mum's only been dead for about two hours."

Margaret said, "It's funny that there isn't any money in her bag. Mum always had money!"

John said, "There are a couple of months left on the leasehold."

I was bemused! I had the feeling that Margaret thought the lodgers might have taken her money. I thought good luck to them if they had but I didn't think for one moment that either of them would do such a thing.

My John said to my brother-in-law, "Come on, let's go into the kitchen and leave the girls to talk. This has nothing to do with us."

My eldest sister, Frances arrived, and she was upset because she had fallen out with Mum, so she had a guilty conscience. My sisters had made their minds up about things they wanted from the house, so I suggested that they paid a small amount of money for anything that they wanted and then it could be shared out when everything was finalised. To my surprise they thought it was a good idea. Frances and Margaret decided to come back the next day.

After they went, I went into my mum's bedroom, which was on the ground floor. The room didn't smell very nice so I opened the French windows. I stripped the bed and found a handbag under the mattress. I put it with the other bag in her wardrobe; I never even looked inside it.

The next morning Frances and Margaret came and we sat in the kitchen. I told them, " I have my typewriter, so I can write any letters we need to."

Frances replied, "What for? You're taking over like you usually do."

I was rather shocked and ended up in tears. It was such an emotional time. I had just thought that I would stay for a few days to give them some help. Pamela was away on holiday at the time.

I went into the front room and told John I wanted to go home.

He said, "Think about it. I'll go and make us a cup of tea."

I went upstairs and started packing. When I came back down, John said, "Are you sure this is what you want to do?" And I did.

Tony came running after us as we went out to the car, saying, "Please will you stay Veronica, for my sake?" And as I told him that I needed to leave, I suddenly remembered that he had bought my mum an engagement ring.

I said to John, "I have to go back to tell Frances and Margaret to make sure that Tony gets his ring back."

On our way home, we stopped at a café which wasn't all that far from where my Uncle George lived so we decided to call on him. Uncle gave me a big hug and I felt a bit better.

A few days later, my nephew rang me to say that my sisters were going to order a wreath, 'The Gates of Heaven'. He asked me if I wanted to go in with them, but I said I'd buy my own flowers.

I didn't want to go to my mum's house before the funeral, but straight to the cemetery. Trevor came with us. When we arrived some of my nieces and nephews came over to speak to us. I had decided that I wouldn't go back to the house after the service, but two of my nieces begged me to go, so I did.

Sometime later, I found out that my sisters had told Raymond and Tony that they would have to find somewhere else to live. They even got the electric turned off, so that they couldn't have any hot water to wash or shave, and also had the phone cancelled. I had planned to go to the council to see if they could be re-housed before they were evicted, and I couldn't believe the way that they were being treated, especially after how much they had done for my mum. Raymond had even slept on the floor in my mum's room, just in case she needed anything in the night!

Chapter Fourteen

John had started to lose weight and felt very tired. I talked him into going to the doctors. Normally we would always go together, but for some reason he went on his own, and when he came home he told me he had diabetes. He was so shocked when the doctor told him, because his grandmother had it and she had to have both of her legs amputated. We were both upset, but I tried to console him by saying that things had moved on a lot since his grandmother had it. The doctor prescribed some tablets and he had to have regular blood tests.

We were moving offices at work and I had a yucca plant, which had grown really tall. We were told that we couldn't take plants with us when we moved so I didn't know what to do with it. I had read in our local paper that the hospital needed some TENS machines to help people with chronic pain. I thought I could sell some raffle tickets if I could find someone who would donate a prize, so I rang several hotels and one manager said he would take the plant and donate a meal for two to include a bottle of wine, for the top prize. The raffle then snowballed a bit because several people donated bottles of spirits for prizes.

It all went really well, and I collected £250 which would go towards several machines.

John continued to feel very tired. There were various incidents, and eventually, on another visit to the doctor, he was told he might be having a heart attack. He was in hospital for three days, and then was on a waiting list for an angiogram. We used private insurance to get the test done sooner, and his appointment came through for the day I had my work Christmas lunch.

On the day of the test, I was anxious to leave the hotel where we were having our firm's Christmas lunch and get to the hospital. When I arrived,

John was sitting on a chair beside the bed.

I said, "How did you get on? I don't suppose you've had the results yet?"

He replied, "Yes, I have to have a triple heart bypass."

I said, "Don't you joke with me!"

He said, "I'm not joking, you ask that man over there."

The other patient confirmed it. I went cold. I hadn't been expecting that news and it was such a shock, especially as it was also the anniversary of my dad's death.

We got an appointment to see a surgeon in Harley Street, London. It really spoilt our Christmas. All we could think about was, "What's he going to say?" It was even more of a worry because John was self-employed, and being a one-man band, he could lose all of his customers. We went to London at the beginning of January 1997 and the specialist said that the reason that John was feeling tired was because of his heart. The operation was arranged for 14 January. John told the surgeon that he wouldn't have it done on the thirteenth (he was superstitious). He went in on the thirteenth and an extra bed was put in John's room so I could stay.

On the morning of the operation, I decided to go and look around the shops, to try to distract myself. John was in the theatre for five hours, and when I eventually went to see him in the intensive care unit, he looked awful, with tubes coming out from several places. While I was there, the anaesthetist came in to check on him. She told me that he had had five bypasses. He was still unconscious, but she said to him, "No more fags John!" The surgeon had never told him to give up, but he did.

The next morning John was moved to the high dependency unit. Some of the tubes had been taken out, so he was looking a bit better. He told me that the nurse had pulled one tube out and that it was very painful.

His friend Paddy came to see him. I asked him not to stay too long because he was in a lot of pain and was very tired. He was on morphine, but it was making him very nauseated. Looking back, I should never have stayed in the same room as him. He was really horrible to me and had me in tears

252

several times. He wasn't a very good patient. He was all right with the nurses, but then he had always been a ladies man; he had a lot of charm! I thought it was a good idea for me to be near him, but I should have stayed at home.

On the day that he had his clips out, he was a bit apprehensive. Some of the veins used in the bypass had been taken from his leg, which had seventy-nine clips. The surgeon had also used the mammary artery in his chest. The nurse started removing the clips on his chest, but when she got to the last few on his leg at the top, they were very painful.

He was going to be discharged on the ninth day, so he asked Trevor to come and take us home. He was the only person who he trusted to drive him. He wasn't a good patient, nor a good passenger. He sat in the car with a pillow in front of his chest to protect him from any bumps that might occur. He was told that he shouldn't go upstairs more than twice a day, but John being John went up more times than that in an hour, even though we had a downstairs toilet.

The next day he was serving a customer off his van, although he didn't actually climb on the van but let the customer do it. After a couple of weeks he asked a friend to deliver some goods for him. He was determined to keep his business going.

He had applied for sick benefit and was sent a payment book with several payments in it, but I told him he couldn't cash them, as even though he wasn't working, his goods were being sold and would have to go through the accounts.

I rang the benefits people to check, and they said that they had never come across a case like it, but they checked and asked us to return the payment book.

I was finding it hard trying to looking after John. He used to get so upset that he couldn't go out to work, and was prescribed tablets to lift his mood. He wasn't allowed to drive for six weeks, but as soon as the time was up, told me he was going to go for a little drive. When I got home from work, he wasn't there and I was worried. When he came in, he told me that he had been to one of his suppliers and had driven eighty miles. I couldn't believe it. Getting back to work was much better medicine than tablets, which he never took anyway.

Chapter Fifteen

In June 1997 I was sixty, which is the age that civil servants normally retired, but I was hoping to work a bit longer, or until I knew how John was going to manage when he started work again. My boss was pleased that I wanted to stay and had no problem making a case to justify me staying on because my section dealt with the BSE crisis.

I arranged to have my photo taken at a photographer's studio, and as a treat I gave one to John on his birthday. He didn't think much of the idea or the photos! We went away for a few days to Swansea, Wales, and as usual John upset me about some trivial thing. I went back to the room and started packing, saying, "I'm going home." We had only been there for two days. He thought I was pretending, but I meant it, so we checked out and returned home.

Veronica 16 June 1997 (age 60)

John's doctor wasn't very keen about signing him back to work eight months after his surgery, but he was determined. I was worried about him because he looked so tired. One evening as he was doing some packing in the garage, I went out to him and suggested, "John, why don't we sell up and move somewhere cheaper? We would have some capital to live on." We had some savings and I knew that we would get a good price for our house.

He said, "No, I'm all right, I like working."

I used to read a magazine called 'Choice' that went around the office on circulation, and, even though I didn't know anything about the area, I had noticed advertisements for very reasonably priced bungalows in Lincolnshire. I put it to the back of my mind.

A few weeks later, John said, "I think you might be right!"

I said, "About what?"

He replied, "About moving."

We discussed it, and decided that we would go to Lincolnshire and have a look at the bungalows. There were quite a lot of new ones but mostly on housing estates. I wasn't very keen on living on an estate but I had always wanted to live in a bungalow. I think it was because I had been happy in the prefab and ground floor flat.

We spent a weekend looking around. We called into an estate agent in Boston and told a young lady what we were looking for. She gave us details of two that were in different villages, and also told us about two that were built by a small builder, that were out in the sticks which sounded interesting.

We went and had a look at them all from the outside, and the following week we made arrangements with the agents to see inside the first two. One was a four-bedroom bungalow, but the total plot was about an acre. It needed a new kitchen, bathroom and boiler. We went to the local pub for lunch and discussed it. I said to John, "We've done lots of renovation before, and we're moving from a house with half an acre, so we don't want to take on more." He agreed.

We went on to see the other bungalow and although it had looked nice from the outside, but the rooms were too small, and it had a septic tank.

On the way home I said to John, "I liked the new bungalows best, can we go and have another look at them, and see if we can contact the builder to have a look inside?" We had just passed the turning, so we turned around and went back.

We managed to contact the builder and he came to show us around the bungalow. We had made a list of all the things that we wanted in our new home. The price of the bungalow included an allowance for the fittings in the kitchen, bathroom and en-suite. There were three bedrooms, lounge, separate dining room, bathroom, en-suite for the main bedroom and a double garage.

The only thing that it didn't have was a utility room, but the bonus was the en-suite. The double garage was at the end of the drive, which was detached from the bungalow. At the back, the garden was a reasonable size, with fields and views to the Lincolnshire wolds. It all felt very spacious.

We had a good look around and liked what we saw. John looked at me to see what my reaction was, and he knew that I wanted it. John said to the builder that we would have it.

The builder, Mr Upsall, said, "I'm not going to take any offers!"

John replied, "I wasn't going to make any offers. We'll pay the full price." It had recently been reduced by £2,000.

The new bungalow 1997

John told Mr Upsall that there were several things that he wanted done as extras, including more electric points. I also wanted the kitchen, bathroom and en-suite fully tiled. We went home feeling very excited, but at the same time wondering what we had done. We had managed to buy the bungalow with our savings, and that took the pressure off John having to run his business down. He didn't want to sell it, because he would worry that the new owner wouldn't serve his customers as well as he did, although he would have loved it if Trevor had taken it over. He would have spent some time with him, to show him the ropes.

The sale took about three months to complete. This was partly our fault because we kept on thinking of other things that we wanted done. Mr Upsall never wrote anything down, but always managed to do what we asked of him.

We had our house in Reading valued and were pleasantly surprised with the valuation. At that time property prices were rising, but until we got the estate agents in, we didn't have a clear idea.

John wasn't very well the weekend that we had to choose the equipment and fittings for the kitchen, bathroom and en-suite, so I had to do it all. It was rather a lot to do in one day, but I managed it.

At this stage we never told anyone that we were buying the bungalow. I didn't even tell my boss at work, as I thought the longer I worked, the money would come in useful for carpets and other necessities. We took possession of the keys on 2 December 1997. John had loaded his van up with the bare essentials, because we wouldn't be moving in for a while, and blinds were fitted on the day we got the keys.

It was very exciting, a new life.

At Christmas, we told Trevor. He was a bit surprised, but knew we were looking. We took him to see the bungalow, and when he walked in he said, "There's nothing that I have seen yet that I don't like."

There was a lot to do ordering carpets, curtains etc. We bought a double bed from our house and some garden chairs to sit on. It was like being on holiday.

Because I worked flexi hours, I took half hour lunch breaks, so that I could save up my time and have every other Friday afternoon off to go to the bungalow. John used to be almost ready when I got home and then we would leave. The journey took just over three hours on a good run. I used to feel guilty asking my boss for the Friday afternoons off, because I still hadn't told him that we had bought our bungalow.

On one of our visits, I was sweeping the lounge floor, which was concrete, and suddenly thought, why don't we let our house out? I went in the other room and said to John, "Why are we selling our house?"

He said, "What do you mean?"

I said, "Why don't we rent it out? That way it will give us an income."

He replied, "Why didn't I think of that!"

The seed had been sown. John had always said that I was his financial adviser. I don't know where I get it from; it certainly wasn't from my upbringing! This plan would give us the choice of moving back if we didn't settle. John was only fifty-seven, so wouldn't have a pension for a few more years. We continued to go to Lincolnshire every other weekend, or longer if we could, for over a year. One of the neighbours, Frank, and his wife Margaret, planted our front garden with flowers and it looked lovely. We would to take them out for a meal or John would buy some compost to say thank you.

My niece, Rosslynn, was getting married and we were invited to her wedding. It was going to be held in Margate. We booked into a hotel which was the same one I had stayed in with Dave. A lot of the guests were going to stay there as it was where the reception was. When we arrived we discovered that it was nothing like when I had stayed there before. The lovely big rooms had been partitioned off to make two rooms. It certainly left something to be desired. The wedding went well, but it was a long time before there was any food, so John had to go out and get something to eat, because of his diabetes. Rosslynn was a bit late getting to the church, because she was just leaving the house when she caught her dress on a nail. She did look beautiful.

From left: Rosslynn, Pamela, Veronica, Claude & Pamela

Chapter Sixteen

John gave up work on 1 April 1999; it wasn't a fool's joke! I think it was the hardest thing he had ever had to do (apart from marrying me). Selling his van was quite a wrench. He had had it from new, and really looked after it. He had to have it re-registered because he had a personalised number plate L1ROC, because his business was called RockJohn. His customers used to pull his leg about it, ribbing him that he must be doing well. He would say to them, "You don't want to deal with a loser, do you?" He had a wonderful repartee with his customers. He always had something to say to anyone. I sometimes wished that I had some of his skills.

I had been at the Intervention Board for twenty-five years in March. I was on the phone, when I suddenly looked up and saw my colleagues in a group, and I was presented with my twenty-five year medal, a bouquet of flowers and a china horse. They knew that I loved horses.

Veronica and Jeremy Rawson (my Boss) 25 Years

I got a phone call from my Aunt Georgina, to say that Uncle George was in hospital, and was very poorly. We decided that we would go and visit him. Trevor wanted to come with us. We were just getting ready to leave, when my niece rang to say that he had passed away. We went to the funeral, and my sisters were there. I also met my cousin, Anne, who I hadn't seen for many years. It was good to see her, but of course it was at such a sad occasion. I will always remember Uncle George. He took my dad's place after he died. He was always so full of fun.

I had decided to give my notice in at the end of April. I was almost sixty-two and we had got the bungalow almost as we wanted it.

I sent out invitations to my leaving celebration, designing a poster on the computer. Most people had to organise their own leaving parties in those days. I had part of the morning off to prepare the food. I like to make my own sausage rolls and other goodies. I had to prepare a speech to respond to my boss's speech. I started off by saying, "This is not my forte."

My boss said, "Or mine."

I went on to say "Thank you all for coming along to see me off the premises."

That prompted a laugh and the rest was made a lot easier. I was presented with some gifts and a large bouquet of flowers. A lot of people turned up and it all went well. One of the senior officers came and when I thanked him, because he was a busy man, he said, "I wanted to come because you are a lovely lady." I felt quite taken back by his praise. You don't forget moments like that!

Sonia: my colleague and Veronica May 1999

The goodies

When I got home, I was shattered. I would miss the people, because I had such a lot of contact with over a thousand staff, but I was ready to retire. It was the beginning of a new chapter in my life. We planned to enjoy ourselves now that we would have a lot more time.

John kept himself busy doing some of the packing. It was something that he excelled at. One day in July he said that we were moving on Friday 6 August. He had made arrangements with a removal company in Boston, as it was cheaper for them to come to Reading than if we booked a local firm.

We phoned a letting agent, someone came to the house to do the rent appraisal, and we were pleasantly surprised at what we could get in rent. Tenants were soon found, but they wanted the house furnished, so we bought new furniture, including a new fridge freezer. They put a six-month clause in the year contract, which meant they could give a month's notice and leave after six.

The day before we were due to move, our next-door neighbours came around with a rose bush and a card to wish us luck in our new home. While they were there, Trevor turned up and I broke down and said, "I hope we are doing the right thing!"

Trevor put his arms around me and said, "Of course you are, Mum." It was all a bit overwhelming!

A bit later that evening, I was in the lounge and John called me to see two fox cubs and two badgers in the garden; it was an amazing sight. We knew there were badgers around, but that was the first time that we had seen them. It was as if they had come to say goodbye. We were really going to miss the wildlife. I just wished that I'd had a camera with me.

The next day the removal van arrived. There wasn't a lot for them to do, because John had done it all. He liked to be in charge. He had got all the things downstairs and into the garage. You would never have thought that he had had a heart operation a few months before. The removal van left and soon after we got on the road.

When we arrived at our bungalow, Red and Doreen, our new neighbours, had put up flags around the front. They had put a sign outside that said, 'They come they go, they come they stay, Welcome.' When we were about to open our entrance door, Doreen passed a plant over the hedge. When we got inside there was a basket of flowers from Frank and Margaret.

We also had cards from other neighbours. After about ten minutes, Red and Doreen brought two trays around with tea, sandwiches, a quiche and a cake. It was overwhelming. We had never experienced anything like it before. I eventually wrote an article for our local paper, which I headed, 'Neighbours from Heaven.' My article got the top position on the letters page.

Arrival day 6 August 1999

We started to get settled in, and decided to go for a walk most mornings before breakfast. It was nice and peaceful here, and apart from a few lorries or tractors, there wasn't a lot of traffic. We had to be aware of any vehicles coming because there weren't any footpaths at that time.

After about two weeks, John got an infection in his leg where his plate was. We went to see the doctor, who wasn't happy with it so he gave us a letter to take to the hospital. He was kept in to have intravenous antibiotics, and his leg settled down.

Living in Boston is like another world. People don't rush around as much as they do in the south. We have some lovely sunsets. The land is very flat and arable. I did miss the trees at first, but realised the bonus of not having to clear the leaves every autumn. While we were in Reading, John used to moan about the squirrels, because they were always eating the bird's nuts, but since the move he was missing them.

Just before the six months was up for our tenants in the house, I rang the agent to find out if there had been any feedback about the six-month clause. I was told that the tenants were very happy and that the children loved their school. The agent spoke to the tenants and then came the bombshell; they wanted to give notice. Because they were in this country for three years, we were given the impression that they would be staying in our house for that time. We wouldn't have spent over three thousand pounds on furniture had we known, but we would have let it unfurnished.

We soon got new tenants, though the rent had gone down a bit. At that time there were a lot of people buying to let. The rent still helped us with our living expenses, because John wasn't receiving his pension yet. It was a really wise move.

Chapter Seventeen

John was going to be sixty in the year 2000. I wrote to some of his friends in London and said that I wanted to arrange a surprise lunch for him, and asking them if they would be able to come. I invited neighbours Red, Doreen, Frank and Margaret. I went to the pub to book the table, which was tricky because John always liked to know where I was going, so I had to do it on a hairdresser day. I sent the menu to his friends, asking them in advance to choose what they wanted, and arranged for replies were to be sent to Red and Doreen's house, so John wouldn't find out. I was very happy with how it was all going.

On the day, a taxi arrived to take us to the pub. As soon as we got there, John looked at the parked cars and said, "That's a Hertfordshire number plate on that car!" You could never really surprise him! We had a great time and came back and had a few more drinks at the bungalow. John couldn't believe that he had reached sixty, because he never thought that he would get past fifty; it must have been the way that I looked after him.

Margaret, Doreen, Redford, Frank and John.

John with friends on his 60th Birthday

In July we booked a short break at a hotel in Morecambe. While we were there, I was looking at the brochures that were in the room, and saw that we were near to the Isle of Man.

When I told John, he said, "Yes I know. When we decide to go, we can stay at this hotel before going."

I said, "No, I want to go now."

He said, "All right then, if you can get booked into a hotel, we'll go." Although he was a bit surprised by what I had said, we were starting to realise we were retired now and should make the most of it while we could.

I booked into a lovely hotel overlooking a golf course for four nights, and we took our car over on the ferry, which was rather expensive, especially as we didn't use it when we were there. I said to John, "Why don't we get one of the freedom passes?" and that is what we did. It enabled us to go around by bus and get on and off when we liked. We liked being there so much that we extended our stay. In one of the villages there was a tin bath race, using the baths that people used to bath in years ago. It was hilarious.

Then we received a phone call from one of our old neighbours, to tell us that another of our Reading neighbours had died, so we decided to go home, to go to the funeral.

Tin bath race Isle of Man 2000

John looking at the scenery Isle of Man

John found retirement hard at the start, and was like a bear with a sore head. After a while he began to accept it, and we used to try and have one day out a week. We would choose somewhere different, and most weeks we would invite Frank and Margaret, who were good company. One year we went to the Lincoln Christmas Market, and to see a Christmas show in Thursford.

John mentioned to the diabetic specialist that he was still feeling very tired and often suffered from nausea. He was told that he could be suffering from a condition called neuropathy, where diabetes damages the nerves in the oesophagus and the bowel. He had a test that came back positive, but there was no treatment. It was awful for me to watch him suffering, knowing that there was nothing that I could do to help him.

In 2001, we were visiting friends in and discussing holidays. John mentioned that he would like to go abroad, but he was too scared of flying. Our friend, Sonia, said, "Why don't you go on a cruise?" We had never even given it a thought. When we got home, we went into a travel agents and began to look at brochures. John fancied Norway, and I didn't mind where we went. We booked a ten day cruise in June.

The tenants in our house made an offer to buy, but we refused because the offer was too low. We had the house valued and we were very surprised to find out it had gone up a considerable amount since the previous valuation. We spoke to the letting agents and they told us that it wasn't easy to rent such a good house as it was a family house and not suitable for people sharing. We decided to put it on the market, and soon had an offer that we accepted.

We went to Reading to remove all the furniture and have a good clear up. Trevor had some of the furniture and friends of his had the rest. Everything was nearly new.

When the day came for us to leave for the last time, I thought that I would be upset, but I wasn't. John had his last walk down the garden; it was a beautiful garden that John had worked hard on. We had enjoyed every minute that we lived there. The garden had been John's life, but we were now entering a new chapter in our lives together and we had no regrets.

Chapter Eighteen

We were looking forward to our holiday in Norway, which was only a few weeks away, when one morning I went to get out of bed and I couldn't walk across the room. My left knee was very swollen and painful. John took me to see the doctor, which wasn't our normal GP. When I was called to go into the doctor's room, John had to help me. Two women were laughing, and John told them that it was nothing to laugh about. The doctor was waiting outside his room. He looked at me and said, "Is this your normal pace?"

I said, "No."

He asked me a few questions and then wrote out a prescription for some tablets without even looking at my knee!

I was feeling really ill so John phoned the doctors, but because it was a weekend he was transferred to the out of hours doctor who was at the local hospital. A doctor came out to see me and after examining me said that I had baker's knee (a fluid filled lump behind the knee). He told me that the tablets had taken the lining off my stomach, so he gave me some different ones. I have since found out that I can't take anything with codeine in.

After a couple of weeks the pain in my knee was still no better, so we went back and saw a different doctor; but still not my regular GP. Again he asked me a few questions and John said, "The doctor she saw last time didn't even look at her knee!"

His reply was, "Well, I haven't yet."

John said, "I think she should have x-rays on her knees because she hasn't had any for a long time."

The doctor then checked my knees and said that I had arthritis. I already knew that because I was diagnosed when I was thirty-nine. He gave me a form to have both knees x-rayed.

When the results came back I was able to get an appointment to see my own doctor, who confirmed that I had arthritis in both knees. John had already made enquiries about a good surgeon, and I knew I could be referred privately because of the health scheme from my civil service job.

In the meantime we were going on our cruise. It was my birthday the day before the cruise, so John booked a room at the hotel for Trevor, so he could join us and we could have a meal together. While we were in the bar having a drink, Jim Davidson walked in with his lady. Trevor said, "Hello Jim," but Jim just gave him a dirty look and walked away. We weren't impressed.

When we boarded the Oriana, we found a lovely bouquet of flowers and a card in our cabin from Trevor. Our cabin had a balcony and everything was great. Before sailing we went on deck where we had champagne and a band played 'We are sailing'. The atmosphere was terrific.

We really enjoyed the cruise and decided to book another one when we got home. Norway is wonderful; the scenery is out of this world, and we were lucky to have good weather. One of the things that I liked about cruising was that once you get to your cabin and unpack, you don't have to touch your cases again until the night before your last day. You just have to put your cases outside the door late at night and you don't see them until you disembark. We had been used to touring where we just lived out of our suitcases.

John and Veronica June 2001.

Flowers from Trevor

John and Veronica Norway 2001

John had been feeling very tired again and when he last had a check-up with his heart specialist, I just happened to mention that he snored a lot, and that it wasn't like normal snoring. Dr Nyman, the heart specialist, said to him, "You might have something called sleep apnoea." This is a condition where the airways get blocked and you stop breathing several times during the night. He said that he would make arrangements for him to see a specialist at Leicester.

We decided to book another cruise to the Canaries in the middle of November. We thought it would be a nice break just before Christmas, and I was really looking forward to it, because I expected it to be nice and warm.

The day had arrived for me to see the surgeon about my knees. We walked in the room and Mr Watson shook hands with us and said, "Well, Mrs McBean, both your knees are shot! The bone is rubbing on bone. You need two new knees!"

I was really shocked. I said, "I thought you were going to do a wash out!"

He replied, "Yes I could do a wash out and you would be back in six weeks. It would be an absolute waste of time."

John said, "You won't do both together will you?"

Mr Watson said, "I can, but it's up to your wife to decide."

I decided to go for it.

John asked, "How long is the waiting list?"

He said, "About eighteen months to two years."

John said, "She's not going to wait that long, we'll pay for it," and joked, "If we pay for one, do we get one free?"

Mr Watson checked his diary and booked me in for 17 September. We found out that if you only have one knee done, there was a fixed price system, no matter how long your stay in hospital was, but having both done together meant there would be an itemised bill.

John and I went to the appointment with the specialist to check if he had sleep apnoea. When we walked in the room and sat down, the doctor said, "Just looking at you, I'm ninety per cent sure you have got sleep apnoea. Two of the most common signs are excess weight and a thick neck. I'll arrange for you to go to the sleep clinic for the night to be monitored." The doctor arranged for him to have the test done the week before my operation. John drove himself there and back. He was told that he had the condition. The only treatment was to wear a mask at night that was attached to a machine that would open up the airways. He found it very hard to keep it on. He would start off all right and then he would pull it off in his sleep. He did feel a bit better after keeping it on for a while, but in the end he gave up.

I had to go for a pre-op check a few days before my surgery. Everything was fine. When I saw the anaesthetist, he said that my list of illnesses that I had provided was very informative. I find it better to keep a record on my computer and print it out when I have to see a specialist, rather than relying on my memory when I get to my appointment.

I was told that I would have to go into the high dependency unit after the operation, but even though I was a private patient, any emergencies would be dealt with first.

The following week I went in for my operation. I had all the usual checks before I went to theatre. When I woke up I was in the high dependency unit. I remember the male nurse telling me that his name was Trevor. I said, "That's good, my son's name is Trevor."

It was very noisy in there so John complained, and was told the staff were having a meeting. John said, "You should have your meeting somewhere else. There are very sick people here." Late that evening I was moved back to the private ward where it was quieter. The next day I walked across the room. My knees were very painful, but I was determined to get moving again. The physiotherapist came the day after my operation and told me what I needed to do. It was a bit frightening at first, because I couldn't even lift my legs off the bed.

I found the hardest thing was losing my independence. The nurses would help me get out of bed by gradually letting my legs down. I knew I was on the road to recovery and getting back to normal again. On the Saturday I had a surprise visit from Trevor and when he was leaving, I walked with him to the exit door. He was very surprised at how far I could walk. Mr Watson used to come in and see me every day. One day he pushed my knees right back and it was very painful.

After eight days I was allowed to go home. John had got a piece of hardboard for me to do my exercises on. I sat on a chair and just moved my legs up and down several times. I did it every hour and gradually got my legs moving.

After six weeks I had to go back to see Mr Watson. When I got up to go into his consulting room, he said, "Well I don't know what you've been doing Mrs McBean, but whatever it is, it's worked, otherwise you would have been walking in here on crutches. You're a good advert."

John told him, "She's done her exercises every hour." Mr Watson was very pleased with me, he told me to carry on with the good work and that he didn't need to see me again. We told him that we had got a cruise booked for two weeks' time, and asked if he thought it would be all right for me to go. He said there was no reason to cancel it and that I would be fine.

The day before we went on our cruise, my hairdresser told me that my neighbours were going on a cruise. I said, "I doubt if it will be the same one that we're going on." When I got home, I said to John, "I'm just going to walk to the post box to post a letter."

When I came back, Doreen came running out and said, "I hear you're going on holiday."

I replied, "Yes, and I understand you are. Are you going somewhere nice and warm?"

She said, "We hope so."

Our cruise was to the Canary Islands on the Aurora. We stayed at a hotel again the night before, because we thought it would take the pressure off getting to the port on time. When we arrived at the port, John arranged a wheelchair for me, and I was taken straight to our cabin. I wasn't able to get off the ship when we docked at several countries, but we had a lovely time. John got off, but he was never gone for long, because he didn't like leaving me. I used to sit on a sun lounger on deck and read a book, it was a bit of a struggle to get up and down, but I made it.

John and Veronica November 2001 on the Aurora

I went to the disabled toilet after breakfast on the first morning, and heard John laugh. When I got outside, John said, "Look who's here!" It was our neighbours, Red and Doreen. Whoever would have thought that they would book the same holiday?

Chapter Nineteen

Our lives seem to be centred around doctors or hospitals. John was having a lot of pain in two of his toes and was diagnosed with a condition called hammertoes, which he had suffered from previously. He needed surgery, and Mr Watson booked his operation for February. It was successful, but soon after one of his pins came loose and had to be pushed back in again.

John would spend a lot of his time in the garden, planting his vegetable seeds and looking after them once they had germinated. He grew runner beans, French beans, onions, shallots, leeks, beetroot, courgettes, lettuce, spring onions and tomatoes. He used to put signs out the front to sell some of the veg that we didn't use. He also gave some to friends, or if we were visiting friends he would take a selection for them. When we had appointments at the hospitals, he would take some for the nurses. He just enjoyed giving and was a very generous man.

Sometime after the shocking twin towers terrorist attack in New York, I realised that I had never told Trevor that I loved him. I'm sure he knew, but I never forget to tell him now. In my day people never expressed their feelings, but it is very important. Hearing about all the firemen that died had a big impact on me, and reminded me again of the terrible news that I had received some years before. Their job is so dangerous because they go in when everyone else is trying to get out.

In 2002, we decided to book two more cruises. One was to the Baltic, Sweden, Germany, Copenhagen, and Russia. The second one was to the Caribbean. The ports of call were, Tortilla, St Lucia, Antigua, and Barbados. It was a way of seeing other countries without flying and was something to look forward to. We would arrive home from the Caribbean nine days before Christmas. John didn't like the heat; so that holiday was going to be for my benefit.

After the operation on my knees, John said that I should get someone to help me with the housework. I wasn't very keen because I had always done everything indoors myself, while John did the garden and any maintenance. I was very domesticated because of my upbringing. John thought of asking a young neighbour, Sharon, who lived two doors away. He invited her in for coffee one morning, and then asked her if she was interested in doing two hours' housework a week, which she was. It did help to have her around, but I never felt comfortable with it.

Sharon had our key to check the bungalow and pick up the post if we were away. Her children Thomas and Hannah were young, and if they were on school holidays they would come and watch the television while Sharon worked. John really enjoyed having them and he would spoil them; he was very good with children! Thomas rang our bell one day, and said, "When I got home my mum wasn't in, so I thought I should come here."

I said, "You did the right thing," and rang Sharon on her mobile, to tell her.

She said, "The children think of your home as their second home." I was pleased that they knew they could always come here.

John liked to do car boot sales at weekends in the summer. Most of the time I went with him, and we both enjoyed talking to people. It was always a very early start though, and one morning I got out of bed while it was still dark, and stubbed my toe on the bathroom door, breaking it. We couldn't do a car boot sale that day, although the weather wasn't very good, so perhaps it was for the best.

The time was approaching for our cruise to the Baltic. During this cruise we went on various trips at our ports of call, some of which were interesting. We were able to get a feel for each country and find out what they were like. I had never wanted to go to Russia, which felt quite oppressive.

One evening on board we met up with some other people, and John ordered some champagne. They wanted to see our cabin because we had a balcony, so I said, "You can come back if you bring a bottle of champagne," which is out of character for me. Too much champagne!

Friends in our cabin 2002

John and Veronica Germany 2002

My retirement plan had always been to write my life history. Some years ago, I was talking to Trevor about something that happened in my life, and he said, "I wish you would write things down, Mum", and that's what gave me the idea. I thought it would help to keep my brain active. When some neighbours told us they were selling their computer as they were upgrading, I told John I'd like to buy it, as it would help me with this project.

It was November, and the time had come for our Caribbean cruise. I was really looking forward to it, because I do like a bit of sun. We had a lot of the time at sea, but there was always plenty going on, so the time went quickly.

We went on some of the shore trips, but were uncomfortable with what seemed to be a very poor lifestyle. We also found the heat overwhelming.

Veronica & John Antigua

Barbados Dec 2002

We arrived home a few days before Christmas. I never really look forward to Christmas and this year Trevor was going to spend it with his girlfriend at her parents' house. We were quite happy about that, but of course we would miss him. Trevor rang us on Christmas Day to wish us a happy Christmas. He said that he felt guilty not coming to us, but I told him he shouldn't. We liked it when he came, but we never took it for granted that he would come.

On Boxing Day we were invited to Keith and Mary's for the evening. We were on our way there when John tripped and fell in the road, – no, he hadn't been drinking. He was carrying an ice bucket that broke. He was more concerned about that than the fact that he had cut his leg. We went back home, I cleaned his leg and put a plaster on it. and we then continued to walk to our friends' place.

We had a pleasant evening, just the four of us, though I was a bit bothered as Keith had a very bad cold. We didn't do anything special; just sat having a drink and a few nibbles and chatting.

When we got up the next morning, I had a bit of a sore throat, and sure enough, I went on to develop a bad cold. We had a quiet New Year's Eve on our own. We received our usual call in the early hours of the morning from Trevor. We always looked forward to that, and it wouldn't be the same if he didn't ring us.

Chapter Twenty

Once again we were making plans for our holidays. John wanted to do Norway again and this time to include Iceland. I fancied the Mediterranean. We decided to do both: Norway in June and the Med in October.

Ever since having the cold after Christmas, which had not completely gone, I hadn't felt right. I didn't say much to John at first, though I knew I was losing weight for no apparent reason. John used to ask me if I had any pain, and I said I didn't. I just felt poorly and seemed to be getting worse. One minute I would be boiling hot and the next shivering.

It got to the beginning of March and I decided to go to the doctor. He examined my chest, but didn't say much except that he was going to prescribe some antibiotics for me. I completed the course but didn't feel any better. John suggested that we go back to see the doctor, so I made an appointment. 2003 was a very hot year with temperatures reaching as high as 100 degrees F.

When I saw my doctor, and told him that I didn't feel any better, he said, "I think I had better send you to hospital."

I said, "What? To stay?"

He replied, "Yes, they will get things moving quicker."

He wrote a letter and told me that I might have to wait a few hours for a bed. We decided to go home first to have a drink and something to eat, not that I felt like eating much.

A doctor came to see me when we got to the hospital. He asked lots of questions and then admitted me. I didn't have to wait too long for a bed; I think about two and a half hours. I was shown to the ward and a nurse listed all the items that I was wearing and that I had brought with me. I had never experienced anything like it before. While she was talking to me, a doctor turned up and said that I had to be put in a side room to isolate me. This was just until they had done some tests on me, to make sure that I hadn't had a recurrence of TB. I wasn't allowed out of the room and had to use a commode, which I hated! The war had just begun in Iraq and the television was full of that, which didn't interest me. I would walk up and down the room to get some exercise, because I was getting some pain in my leg, and I didn't want to get a thrombosis. The days were very long and no one seemed to be doing much. I found out that the doctor who I was under was on holiday for two weeks. Eventually, I had another doctor come and examine me and ask me a few questions.

One night I woke up and I thought I could see little things crawling up the wall. I can't see much without my glasses on, so I put the light on and then my glasses. I got out of bed and went over to the sink, where I saw a lot of ants around the sink and crawling up the wall. I was horrified. When John came in to see me, he went and reported it to the nurse. She told him that there was nothing that could be done, because I wasn't allowed to leave the room, so she couldn't arrange for the room to be fumigated. The next day, John bought in some ant powder and put it around the sink; no one said a word!

Just before I was admitted to hospital, we received the renewal for our private insurance. I was rather shocked at how much it was going up. The policy was in my name, because I got a Civil Service discount. I hadn't realised that when I reached sixty-five, the discount would drop from forty to twenty-five per cent. I decided to cancel the cover. John wasn't very happy about me doing it, but I went ahead and cancelled the standing order at the bank.

My policy payment was due on 1 April for the new amount, and I was admitted to hospital on 31 March. I had been in hospital for about two days when I thought, what have I done? I lay awake all night thinking about it. When I got up in the morning I checked in my handbag for my address book, to see if I had the BUPA telephone number in it, and luckily I did. Soon after nine in the morning I rang. I explained to the lady that I had been a bit hasty, because I had got a bit worked up about the increase. She said, "I will see if I can restart it for you." And she did. I was so grateful.

When John came in to visit me, I told him what I had done. He said, "Good, I didn't want you to cancel it, but I didn't say too much because I knew that you weren't very well. Even if we have to use our savings, we'll still pay into it." I felt a weight had been taken off my shoulders.

About two weeks into my stay in the hospital, a physiotherapist came to give me some exercises. She was very abrupt and I ended up in tears. Some of the things that she was asking me to do were just impossible. The results of my TB tests had come back negative. I asked the Doctor if I had pneumonia, and he said that he was still trying to find out. There was talk of me being moved out on to the main ward, but it didn't happen. At least I was able to leave the room and have a walk about. There were two elderly ladies who were crying out for a nurse, but no one went near them. I went in to help one of them who was trying to reach her handbag. It upsets me to see elderly people treated like that.

I saw the doctor once after he came back from his holiday, and he discharged me. A follow-up appointment was made for a month's time. I had been in hospital for three weeks and discharged without a diagnosis, and John wasn't very happy, so we decided to go private. Things soon started to move after that. The specialist arranged for several tests including a CT scan. It was getting near to the time when we would be going on our cruise to Norway, so I asked if it would be all right for me to go. The doctor assured me it would. Looking back now, it was the wrong advice.

About this time, Trevor was thinking of changing his job; still as a mechanic, but with a different company. He had two interviews and was offered the job. There was one problem: he had been having a lot of trouble with his knees, and needed an operation on both. John and I offered to pay for it privately, so that he could get it done more quickly, and he accepted our offer. The firm agreed to keep the job open for him until he had his operation.

I went for the first test that I had to have done at the hospital. After a long wait for the results, the doctor finally appeared and took us to his room. He told me that I had got a blood clot on my left lung, and that he needed to get me booked into the warfarin clinic immediately. I needed to go straightaway and find out what strength tablets I should have.

I was due to have a CT scan the next day, and when I arrived told the radiologist that I had been diagnosed the day before with a blood clot on my left lung. She said, "In that case it is very unlikely that you have got what the doctor is looking for. Do you still want the scan?"

I said that I did. We were due to go on the cruise in 6 days so I rang to get an appointment for the results before we were due to leave.

That evening I decided to try on some of my cruise clothes but nothing fitted. John took me to Grantham, where there is a large shop selling designer clothes at reduced prices but I was unlucky and couldn't find anything. John then took me to Peterborough, and I managed to get a few things there. I had lost such a lot of weight and hadn't thought about my clothes not fitting me.

When we walked into the specialist's office, he was on the phone and doing something on the computer at the same time. We felt that we were intruding. He just blurted out, "You've got a tumour on your bronchia." I was rather stunned, but not surprised. He continued, "You'll have to have a bronchoscope, so that a biopsy can be done." This procedure is a tube going down from the mouth into the lung, and I had known about it when I was in hospital with TB. John didn't seem to take it all in. I asked again if it was all right for me to go on holiday and he said it was.

When we got outside, John said, "Did he really say that you have got a tumour?" and I told him he was correct.

I struggled to do the packing, because I really didn't feel well. I was secretly thinking, "I wish we weren't going!" I didn't want to spoil it for John, because he was looking forward to the cruise.

Veronica John, Norway

I was feeling very poorly and began to wish that we had cancelled, but I never even thought about whether our insurance cover would be valid if I had to be admitted to hospital. We enjoyed the cruise as much as we could.

I had to see a chest specialist at the local hospital to arrange for the test and biopsy to be done. Trevor had come to stay for the weekend and I had a private word with him. I said, "Trevor if anything should happen to me, there are two things that I want to say to you, one is, please keep in touch with John."

He said, "Of course I will, Mum!"

"The second is, don't grieve for me for as long as you did for your dad."

He gave me a big hug.

Trevor came to the hospital with us. The specialist, Dr Clifton, didn't see private patients, so I saw him on the National Health. That day I was feeling terrible, one minute I was cold and the next very hot. The temperature was high for that time of year. When we went into see Dr Clifton, he had two students with him. John asked him if I had got cancer. He said, "Everyone thinks because they have got a tumour, that it is cancer." John took an instant dislike to him, and said he was playing to an audience.

I was supposed to have had the bronchoscope the next day, but when I told him I was feeling terrible he sent me for an x-ray. I then had to be called back in for the results, and he told me, "You can't have the bronchoscope tomorrow, because you've got pneumonia." I had to go for some blood tests and an appointment was made for me to see him the following week. When I went back he said that the test was arranged for the next day.

When I arrived at the hospital, I was a bit nervous: although I'd had a good few tests in my life, I'd never had this one. The doctor gave me a sedative so I didn't remember much about it.

The doctor confirmed to John and I that I had a tumour and that I needed surgery, but he was unable to do the biopsy, because it would be too difficult. John asked if I could be referred to the Royal Brompton Hospital in London, because that is where I went when I had TB. The hospital had been given the Royal title because Princess Margaret had her lung operation there. They got me better before, and hopefully they would again.

We had to wait a long time to see the surgeon, Mr Goldstraw. He told me that I had a very rare tumour, called a carcinoid tumour. The doctors don't know what causes it and it's not easy to diagnose. He said that it had to be removed. I would have to be admitted five days before the operation to run all the tests again, including the bronchoscope, but this time under general anaesthetic. A friend of ours, Nell, very kindly said that we could stay with her the night before I went into hospital.

A few months before, I had been looking in a jeweller's window at some Swarovski glass, and saw a horse and a fowl. John and I had given up buying each other gifts for our birthdays, but I said, "I would like that for our silver wedding anniversary next year." He decided to buy it that year. I think he was worried in case I wouldn't get over the operation.

Trevor asked me if I wanted him to let Linda know about my illness. I said, "No, I don't want her coming to see me because she thinks I am dying." It was emotional enough as it was. We arrived at Nell's the night before I went into hospital. We parked our car on a meter and displayed my disabled parking badge. The next morning we found that we had got a £50 fine. We hadn't realised the parking rules were different in London.

When we arrived at the hospital, I was taken straightaway to the old part of the hospital, where I had been an inpatient in 1955.

John took the car to Reading and parked it on a friend's drive, returning to London by train. He then got taxis from Nell's place to visit me in hospital.

My sister, her husband and my nephew came to visit me on the Saturday and then Nell and her daughter arrived. It got a bit crowded and noisy. I was a bit concerned about other patients. In the end, Nell, Robbie and Peter decided to go for a walk. They ended up in a pub. Peter and Robbie started a relationship after that.

I decided to go to Mass on the Sunday; I hadn't been for several years but I spoke to the priest after the service, and told him about my operation, he said he would pray for me. That afternoon, one of my nieces came to see me, bringing me a Bible and some other leaflets. She said a prayer out loud for me, which I felt a bit uneasy about at first, but it was very touching, and John felt the same.

I went to visit the chapel in the hospital, and on the way there I looked at a plaque listing consultants that had worked in the hospital. I found the name of the consultant, Dr Livingstone, who looked after me when I had TB. It made me feel at home.

The chapel was very peaceful, but then I heard some bells ringing. Unsure of where the sound was coming from, I went out and realised that it was a fire alarm and was told to wait outside. When I saw the fire appliance arrive, I started to panic as I still get very upset when I see them. Returning to my room, I shed a few tears, but then I had the sense that Dave was coming to wish me luck for my operation.

Mr Goldstraw came to see me on the Monday morning, and said, "Instead of doing your bronchoscope tomorrow and the operation the next day, I can do both tomorrow, because whatever the results, the tumour has to be removed." I was also asked if I would agree to being glued together internally, which was a new trial. I agreed and had to sign my consent.

John asked him what the risks were of the operation. He said, "Do you mean death?" He explained, "There is always a risk for any operation, but if your wife was in her seventies (I was sixty-six) the risk would be a lot higher."

I was given a pre-med at 7 am, but I didn't go to the theatre until 2 pm. The next time that I knew anything I was in the intensive care unit. John had been to the church opposite while I was in theatre. He saw some people in there, but he couldn't speak to them; he was so worried about me.

The next morning I had some of the tubes removed, but I had two big drains that came out of my lung. The nurse came along and told me that I was going back to my room; she was expecting me to walk, and she was also talking about me going on an exercise bike. I had just had three quarters of my lung removed, and didn't feel strong enough for any of that. John asked for a wheelchair and took me to my room. The temperature was over a 100 degrees F, and there was no air conditioning in the room, even though it was in the private wing.

The registrar had told me to walk around a certain area every hour to exercise my lung, which I did, but it seemed that every time he came to the ward, I would be resting on the bed. My niece, Rosslynn, came to visit me one day, and while she was there the doctor came in and had a go at me. Rosslynn told him to stop treating me like a child. I told him that I had been walking about every hour like he told me to, but I don't think he believed me. I had to go to another floor every day to have a chest x-ray. That made me very out of breath. By the time I got back to my room, the doctor would have received the results electronically; it was amazing.

That weekend, Trevor came to see me. He seemed a bit down, so I asked him if he was all right. He said that he was worried about me, and about his new job and his operation, but finally he told us that his girlfriend had gone back to her parents.

The day came for me to go home. John had to go to Reading first, to collect the car. He brought a pillow for me to put in front of my chest, just in case he had to brake suddenly. I said my goodbyes to the staff, and we left a cheque for their Christmas fund. Before I left the hospital, I asked the doctor if the tumour was cancerous. He said it wasn't, but I have found out since that it was.

Once we were home, John got me settled and then got some food ready. I began to walk around the bungalow a few times a day, then I would walk along the road, increasing it a bit every day. I would walk so far and if there was a seat along the way, I would sit for a while before returning.

When I went back for my check up, Mr Goldstraw asked me how I had been getting on. When I told him about my walks and that I sat down part of the way, he said, "No, I don't want you to sit down when you get out of breath, I want you to get the bit of lung you have got left working!"

I continued to feel a bit stronger each day, and started to do some things around the bungalow. Mr Goldstraw had said to me one day, "Looking at your health record, it is a wonder that you're still around."

We had to cancel our next cruise. We had a terrible job to get our money back. I had to make several phone calls and a form was sent to my doctor, who had to log all the appointments that I had with him during a certain period, stating what they were for. We eventually got our money back less the excess, until I spoke up about all the trouble I had getting a refund, when they paid in full.

By this time Trevor had had his operations and started his new job. He seemed to be a lot happier.

Chapter Twenty-One

After Christmas and at the beginning of 2004, John told me he had an infection behind the plate in his leg, and had noticed pus coming out for a while. He hadn't gone to the doctor before now, because he knew I wasn't very well. The doctor put him on antibiotics, but it didn't improve, so he was referred to an orthopaedic surgeon, Mr Watson.

Once again, we used our private insurance, so didn't have to wait for long. He had stronger antibiotics, but was no better, so Mr Watson decided to admit him to hospital to have intravenous antibiotics. He was in hospital for a few days. John had always dreaded that he might have to have the plate taken out of his leg one day; it had been in for over forty years.

When we went back to see Mr Watson, that is exactly what he suggested. I could see the tears in John's eyes, and I was sitting across the room to him, so I couldn't even hold his hand. Mr Watson arranged a date for him to be admitted, and I thought to myself, what else can go wrong? It seemed like nothing but doctors and hospitals ever since we retired.

In April it was our silver wedding anniversary. John had booked a table for dinner at a nearby hotel. When we arrived we were surprised to see a lovely flower arrangement on our table from a friend in Reading. I don't know how she found out where we were going. We had some silver serviette rings and bookmarks from Trevor, and Audrey and Jim sent us a little Swarovski bell on a mirror.

John and Veronica Silver Wedding 2004

Bouquet of flowers

In June, John went into hospital feeling very apprehensive. I didn't dare say anything to him, or he would explode; he wasn't taking the news very well. He had the operation and everything seemed to go all right. Mr Watson had a job to get the plate out, and had to go out to buy a special tool to do the job. John asked to see it afterwards. He was in hospital for his birthday. When he came home he had daily visits from district nurses to dress the wound. There was one part that didn't seem to be healing, so he had to go back into hospital for more intravenous antibiotics. Once again, he came home and the nurses came daily. The leg wasn't healing very well and one part was still very painful.

By this time, we were into October. I rang the hospital and explained what was wrong, and the nurse told me to take him to see our GP, but I insisted we needed to see Mr Watson, who arranged to see him and have a scan. John had an abscess, and needed immediate surgery.

John's best friend, Jimmy, was getting married the following week, for the third time. We were invited but we were unable to go. When John came home it was back to the nurses coming in again. His leg was taking a long time to heal. He had to take more antibiotics for three months, and even then his leg was still very painful every time he put any weight on it.

That Christmas, we decided to go away to a hotel called The Papworth, at Woodhall Spa. It wasn't too far to drive. It had been used as the officers mess for the famous Dambusters 617 Squadron, who at the time were based at nearby RAF Woodhall Spa. There was a lot of memorabilia from that period, and behind the bar there is the branch of a tree that had been impaled in the fuselage of a Lancaster.

We had a suite overlooking the lovely grounds. We had a choice of going to the races or to see a pantomime, Cinderella, in Lincoln, on Boxing Day. I chose the pantomime. I hadn't been to one since the children were small. It turned out to be the best choice, as the racing was cancelled because of bad weather; it was very cold and icy. We had a great time, but there was some terrible news on the television on Boxing Day, when we learnt about the Indian Ocean tsunami that killed so many people.

John needed crutches to get around, and told Mr Watson that his leg was still very painful, and it was shaped like a banana. Mr Watson referred him to a Professor Harper, at the Royal Infirmary Leicester, on the NHS. We had a terrible job trying to find the hospital. When we arrived for the appointment, Professor Harper looked at John's leg and said, "I think I know what is wrong. You have got a non-union bone that has never healed." He was very abrupt, and gave him two choices: one to have the leg amputated, or the second to have an Ilizarof frame fitted. This is a metal frame with metal rods going into the leg with nuts that have to be tightened every day. The diseased bone would be cut away and a break would be made at the tibia near the kneecap, so that the bone could grow. His leg had always been three quarters of an inch shorter than the other one since his motorbike accident. He always had to have his shoe built up because it affected his back.

Professor Harper said that he would arrange for him to have a scan on his leg. I asked him he could advise in the meantime how to make it a bit more comfortable. He said, "If you wait outside, I will arrange for you to have a cast fitted." He started talking into his dictaphone before we had even left the room, which I thought was a bit rude.

When we got outside, John said, "I think I'll have my leg amputated."

I went cold, and tears came to my eyes. I said, "John, please think about it!"

The sister from the plaster room called us in. When John told her that he thought he might go for the amputation, she told him that he would have a seventy per cent chance of the operation working and that it was worth thinking about it. He had the scan a few weeks later, and we saw Professor Harper after that. John decided to have the operation for the frame, so he was put on the waiting list.

John spent a lot of time researching the Ilizarof frame, and made some enquiries by email, receiving a lot of information.

John had an endowment policy that had just matured, and we decided to buy a new Tempur bed that moulds to your body – I think they are called memory foam these days. With some of the money we decided to go to Scotland for a break. We knew that we wouldn't be able to do a lot, because John was on crutches. I booked a couple of hotels and we booked the rest as we went along. We had a great time and were away for over three weeks.

This year John was sixty-five. I rang his friend's wife, Jennifer and invited them for the weekend and booked a table at a restaurant. John didn't know they were coming until they arrived at the bungalow. Trevor also joined us. We had a most enjoyable evening. It was nice for John because he had been a friend of Jimmy's for a very long time.

John & Veronica (John 65)

Jennifer & Jimmy

299

I was not very happy about John going into the hospital at Leicester, because they had a high level of MRSA infections. I did some research and found someone in Oxford who specialised in the Ilizarof operation. He had operated on some of the people who were blown up in Northern Ireland. His name was Mr McNally. John and I discussed it and asked our doctor for a referral. It was a long way to go, but we felt that it was worth having a second opinion. We decided to use our private insurance and we got an appointment in August.

When we arrived at the hospital for the appointment, we met Mr McNally, who was very charming. He agreed with Professor Harper's diagnosis that the bone was diseased (osteomyelitis). He told John that there was a very good chance that the operation would work. John asked about his age, and he answered, "I have done this operation on an eighty year old man."

John also asked, "How many of these operations do you do?"

He replied, "I do ninety out of the hundred that are done at this hospital every year."

What Professor Harper hadn't told us was that John would have to have a muscle and skin graft taken from the other leg, because there wasn't much flesh over the bone on his leg. The operation would be done by two surgeons, Mr McNally and a plastic surgeon, and would take nine hours. It was a daunting thought, and we could only pray that it would work! He was told that the frame would be on for about six months.

Mr McNally said that he would have to liaise with Mr Critchley, the plastic surgeon, and find a day the theatre would be free; and this was arranged for 28 November.

We had been invited to the 'Gold Card Weekend' at a hotel in Bridlington. We used to get these invitations twice a year, in the spring and the autumn. We never understood why we got invited, but found out at a later date that all the visitors who were at the hotel when the owners celebrated owning the hotel for fifty years were invited back. It was a four day break, and on the Sunday we would be taken on a mystery tour by coach, included in the price.

We decided to go, and enjoyed the break, though we kept thinking about the operation.

Our friends, Audrey and Jim said that I could stay with them when John had his surgery, as the hospital was about thirty miles from Reading.

When John, Trevor and I arrived at the hospital, we were all feeling a bit emotional and apprehensive. Lots of doctors came to see John and the anaesthetist came to discuss what anaesthetic he should have. She recommended that he have an epidural (a needle inserted in the spine). He wasn't very keen on having it, but when she explained that he wouldn't have any pain directly after the operation, and that she would numb the part where the needle went in, he decided to go for it. The operation was to be done the next day, and everything went well.

I went to visit John the next day and found him very bright, saying that he wasn't in any pain. He had a heater blowing on his leg, because of the skin and muscle graft which are living parts. The leg was covered up, and had a little peephole, so that the grafts could be monitored. Mr Critchley told him that if the grafts weren't successful, he would have to go back to theatre and have grafts taken from the top of his back.

I went to visit every day. He was in bed for a few days and the pins in his leg had to be cleaned every day. I used to clean the locker, the table and anything else around him, because I was scared he would get an MRSA infection. He was discharged after three weeks, although he found it very painful when he first put his foot to the floor, but at least the grafts worked, and he didn't have to go back to the theatre. Once again the only person who he wanted to take him home was Trevor, and that meant that I was going to have to drive myself home, which concerned me as I hadn't driven any long journeys for a few years, because John always wanted to be in the driving seat.

The hospital had arranged for district nurses to come in every day to clean the pins, and we spent a lot of time making sure that towels and linen were all kept spotlessly clean. After a few weeks John decided that I could clean the pins as well as the nurses, so they didn't come as often. He got an infection a few times, and the doctor came to see him and put him on antibiotics.

Chapter Twenty-Two

The start of 2006 saw us having check-ups at Oxford on a regular basis. We travelled by taxi because John wouldn't let me drive him, and we got quite friendly with the driver. I carried on cleaning the pins and we just went from day to day. When John got an infection in his leg, the doctor would come to visit him, as it would have been too risky to wait in the waiting room at the surgery where he might have picked up something worse.

I was in town one day and saw a laptop that was on offer. I rang John and told him about it, and he told me to get it. John was spending a lot of time playing cards on the computer so this meant I was able to set up a network, and could access my files on the desktop.

The months went by and we reached the six months after surgery, hoping that the frame would be removed, but the bone hadn't grown enough and still had a little way to go. John took it all in his stride. Mr McNally used to show us the x-rays, and it was amazing to see the results. John was handling it very well, and our friends used to remark on how good he was. It wasn't easy for him having the frame on twenty-four hours a day. He still managed to do a few things in the garden and garage and liked to be kept busy.

John had some routine blood tests done at the doctors that showed he was a bit anaemic. He was referred for an endoscopy (a camera from the mouth into the stomach). He had it done and the results were clear, no cancer. John was over the moon!

I had been experiencing numbness in my little and ring finger on my left hand. I went to see the doctor, and he diagnosed ulnar nerve compression. The cause was the arthritic bone in my elbow pressing on the nerve and I was told operations weren't always successful.

When we next went to Oxford, John asked his specialist if he could recommend someone who specialised in hands, and I went to see Mr Burge, who confirmed my doctor's diagnosis. He told me that he couldn't promise to improve it, but that he wanted to try and stop it from getting any worse. I couldn't have a general anaesthetic, because of my lung but I was sedated, so didn't feel anything. When Mr Burge came out to see me after, he said it went very well, but that it was a mess in there, meaning the arthritis damage.

An appointment was made for John to have his frame removed in December; it had been on a year by then. Although John had been driving to Oxford for the last few appointments, Trevor drove this time. After we settled John in the ward, I had to go for a check up on my arm, as Mr Burge had kindly made the appointment for the same day, and saw me at the same hospital. When I came out, Trevor suggested that we went for a drive to a designer outlet just outside Oxford while we waited for John to have his procedure, but John rang to say that he was ready to go home, saying that the frame had not been removed as the bone still wasn't ready.

A new date was arranged for January. This time we booked into a hotel for two nights. John drove down the day before, and to the hospital the next day. This time the frame was removed, and I drove back to the hotel, though John insisted on driving home the next day. He still had to use his crutches, because he couldn't put too much weight on his leg. His leg was still a bit shorter than the other one, so he would still have to have his shoe built up. Now that the frame had been removed from John's leg, we thought that we might be able to get our lives back on track. We'd had over three years of continuous health problems and it was time things changed.

After a few weeks, John started to feel very tired and cold. He had lost his appetite and developed a pain in his side. We went to the doctors and he was sent for a chest x-ray, which we thought a bit strange when the pain was in his side. The results came back clear. A few weeks later he saw a different doctor, who told him the pain was due to the way he was walking; he was still using crutches.

John was due to have his heart check up with Dr Nyman in April, who immediately noticed John's weight loss, and examined him. He said that he thought his liver was enlarged, and that he would make arrangements for him to have an ultrasound. The scan revealed that the spleen was enlarged. He said that he would arrange for him to have a CT scan, and then referred him to the blood specialist, Dr Sobolewski, who told him that he didn't think the spleen was enlarged, but that he would do some special blood tests. These were normal.

John suggested that we go to Kent to see two of my sisters, and then to see two of my friends: Maureen, who lived in Bognor Regis, and Eileen, who lived in Crawley, Sussex, with her husband, Bert. I thought it was all a bit strange, but I could read him like a book, and I knew that he didn't think he was going to be around for long.

We booked into a hotel for three nights, which was between where my sisters and my friends lived. I had just finished the first volume of this book, 'My Childhood Days,' and I took a copy for each of my sisters. When I gave Frances her copy, she was ripping the envelope open. John said, "Be careful! Veronica has spent a lot of time writing that." It was nice to see everyone, but a tiring few days.

When we got home, John went for his CT scan which showed that the liver spleen and kidneys were normal, but there was something sinister looking in the abdomen. The radiographer suggested that the endoscopy be repeated, so we went back to Dr Fairman, the general specialist who had done one the previous August, and had told us there was no cancer. Dr Fairman came out after the endoscopy was done, and I could see from his face that all was not well. John was still very sleepy, so didn't understand what was going on. We never did receive the results this time.

On the evening of 18 May, we received a phone call from one of my nieces, Benita, who lives in Louth, Lincs. She said, "I've got some bad news, Pamela has died." I was really shocked. I was expecting her to say that my brother-in-law had died, because he was a lot older than my sister. Apparently, she had been to the doctors in the afternoon, and she told him she had a pain down her arm and her stomach was bloated. He told her to go home and take her tablets. A few hours later, she had a massive heart attack and a seizure. She was dead by the time the ambulance arrived. We tried to get hold of my sister, Frances, and eventually got her on her mobile. She couldn't take it in. We were all very shocked. John got me a drink to try and calm me down.

We had a message on our answer machine asking us to make an appointment to see Dr Sobolewski, which we thought was a bit strange because he had already told John that his blood tests were alright. John made the appointment for 7 June. The date for my sister's funeral was three days before.

I managed to book into a Travelodge for two nights, not far from Broadstairs where my sister lived. Trevor said that he would travel down on the morning of the funeral.

John wasn't feeling very well, but still insisted doing the driving. We booked into the Travelodge and then went to see my brother-in-law and family. They were all devastated. I kept thinking how strange it was that John had taken me to see my sister about three weeks before. It was as if I was meant to say goodbye.

We all arrived at Claude's the next day for the funeral. The walls in the lounge were covered in memorial cards; eventually there were about three hundred. I went in one of the main cars with my other two sisters. One of my niece's husbands was taking photos of the funeral procession, which I found distasteful. There were a lot of the public standing all along the high street, because Pamela was so well known in Broadstairs. When we arrived at the church, it was packed with mourners.

Some of the family were taking photos inside the church, which I felt uncomfortable about. I accept that we all do things a different way, and you can't please everyone. The service was very long, because it was a full mass. We all gathered outside to look at the flowers, and speak to people. I was a bit concerned about John, so I told Trevor to take him straight to the hotel. There was no point in him standing there getting cold.

Claude had done my sister proud. There was plenty of food and drinks, and the children had made a video of pictures of Pamela. We met Raymond, the man who used to live with my mum. We stayed the second night in the Travelodge. I had a migraine the next morning, but we thought we should go to see Claude and the family before we went home.

We arrived at the hospital on the Thursday for John's appointment with Dr Sobolewski. He started talking about all the things he had told us on the last visit. He seemed a bit confused. John then asked him if he had the results of his endoscopy. He checked the computer, but there was nothing on it. He then rang to speak to his secretary, and asked her to check. A few minutes later she brought a printout of the results. He read it and then said, "You've got cancer of the oesophagus!" It was like a bomb had hit us. We were both stunned. We knew something was wrong, but we weren't prepared for this, especially after being told the August before that there was no cancer! The doctor was so blunt, but then I don't suppose there is any easy way of telling a patient; it's just a job to them. I always felt that it must have been missed the year before.

John had an appointment the following week to see Dr Nyman, but in the meantime things went drastically wrong. John decided that he wanted to do a car boot sale on the Sunday. I wasn't very keen, but I didn't want him doing it on his own, so I said I would go with him. On the Saturday morning, he loaded my car up with things. He came in to have some lunch, and then decided to have a rest on the bed before loading his car.

After a couple of hours, I heard him shout out, and when I went into the bedroom, he said, "I've got a terrible pain in my leg, not the one that has been operated on." He said it wasn't cramp but the pain was so intense, he couldn't stand on it. I rang NHS Direct and explained what had happened, and they called an ambulance and took John to A&E, with me following in my car.

After a long wait, he was examined and admitted with a diagnosis of an aneurysm, which is very serious.

He had been put under the care of Dr Nyman, who had arranged for him to have a private consultation with a consultant in Leicester about his cancer. It was my seventieth birthday the week after John was admitted to hospital. He had booked a table at a restaurant, and Trevor was coming for the weekend. He asked Dr Nyman if he could come home for the weekend and was told that as long as he was back in hospital first thing on Monday morning, he could go.

On Saturday morning, I went to the hairdressers, and when I got home, Trevor was there and he had brought our good friends, Audrey and Jim with him as a surprise. John had organised this without me knowing. We had a good evening at the restaurant, and the proprietor played his guitar for me. John went back to hospital on the Monday morning.

After a couple of weeks we had to go and see the specialist in Leicester. Because it was a private appointment, I had to arrange transport, so I contacted Alan, the man who used to take us to Oxford, and he said he would take us. The appointment was early evening. We were both on edge when we went into the consulting room. The specialist looked at John's notes, and he told him that he wasn't prepared to operate because of all the things that he had wrong with him. He said that normally the operation would be a ten per cent risk, but with John it would be twenty-five per cent. He said, "Do you want to go through horrible radiotherapy or chemotherapy?" I asked what the prognosis was if he didn't have anything done. He replied, "Six months." John had to go back to the hospital, and we were all very upset, including Alan; he didn't know what to say! We arrived back at the hospital after ten thirty, so we had to ring the bell for security to let us in. Once we got back to the ward, I stayed with John for a while, but he was worried about me getting home. On the way out, one of the nurses spoke to me, and I just broke down. She tried to comfort me. I was very upset driving home, and couldn't get to sleep when I went to bed.

John saw the vascular surgeon about his leg, and he told him that he wouldn't do the main operation, because it was too risky. He suggested one that would leave his leg permanently stiff. At first he agreed to have it done, but when he told me, I advised him to think about it, because it would really affect his life. It would be difficult for him to sit on the toilet, and he wouldn't be able to drive. He booked an appointment for us to see the surgeon together. He told him that he had changed his mind and that he didn't want it done.

Dr Nyman saw John in the ward twice a week. When John told him what the specialist had said in Leicester, he said, "You have got a one in four chance of survival, which is quite good." He didn't tell him to have it done, but implied it was worth a chance. However, John had already decided that he wouldn't have it done; it was such a big operation.

He was in the hospital for several weeks and nothing seemed to be happening. He did go to see the oncologist, who told him that he wouldn't give him chemotherapy or radiotherapy, because his kidneys were damaged. We didn't like his attitude. He wouldn't allow me to say anything, and I had never encountered anything like that before. When John told Dr Nyman what he said, he assured him that there was nothing wrong with his kidneys. He suggested that he saw Mr Beggs, the surgeon from Nottingham, who did the type of operation that he needed. He came to the local hospital once a month. He was put on the list to see him on his next visit. When he came, he told John that he would give him a ninety per cent chance of survival, so he decided to have it done. He then had to wait for a bed at the City Hospital in Nottingham. We were told they had a patient hotel, and I could stay there if there was a free room.

John had been in hospital for six weeks when I got a phone call from him to say that he was being transferred to Nottingham that afternoon, and that I could go in the car with him. I quickly put a few things in a case, and my friend took me to the hospital, to save me leaving my car there, because I didn't know how long we would be away. The driver took John to his ward, and once I found out what the visiting hours were, he took me to the hotel, which was just a ten minute walk from the hospital.

The room was very comfortable, with a walk in shower, and my room rate included breakfast in the restaurant. It was open for lunch between twelve and two, and then again for a hot meal between five and seven. Everyone was so kind and helpful. They even had a laundry service at a very reasonable price, and you could have the use of an ironing board and iron. I was able to keep John's clothes washed, and I was able to visit him three times a day.

John's operation was arranged for the Tuesday after he was admitted. He was ready from early morning, and at three in the afternoon, the doctor came and told him that they had run out of operating time. Mr Beggs came to see him the next morning, and told John that he was supposed to be going on holiday, but if he could get an anaesthetist, he would come in and do the operation on the Friday, so we had a bit of a wait. There was one man in his ward, Ernie, whom he got really friendly with. He had had the same operation, but he didn't have cancer.

The operation was to go ahead. We were both very uptight about it. I went to the ward on the Friday morning, 14 August, to be with him until he went to the theatre. I kissed him before he went and felt sick with worry. To try to distract myself, I got a taxi into Nottingham, but I couldn't concentrate on anything, so soon got a taxi back, and went to my room for a rest. After a while, I rang the intensive care unit to find out if John was out of theatre. The nurse who answered the phone asked me to leave it a bit longer before I visited him. She said he was literally just coming through the doors.

I left it for another hour, but when I got there I wasn't prepared for what I saw! John was screaming and throwing his arms all over the place. The nurse asked me to wait outside the curtains, and said, "We're trying to get his pain relief sorted out." He told me that in all his years of nursing, he had never seen anything like it, and if it wasn't sorted out soon, he was going to do a written report. He said that John should never have left the recovery room. It turned out that the epidural had come out, and he had nothing for the pain. He had just had his oesophagus and half his stomach removed. He had to have another epidural inserted, and then he settled down.

I could visit at any time, so I spent most of my days with him. Trevor and his friend were in Nottingham that weekend to see the cricket, which they'd already arranged before knowing about John's operation. They came to visit him and were a bit upset to see him like he was. John managed a bit of banter with Chris; they got on really well. They took me for an Indian meal in the evening, which was a nice change from hospital meals.

After a few days, John was moved back to the main ward. There was a high dependency unit at the end of the ward, where the nurse could keep an eye on one or two patients. He ended up having four epidural needles in the end, and they all came out. It was a job to find anything to help him with his pain. One day the anaesthetist came to see him, and John said to him, "Don't come anywhere near me. I don't want you to touch me!" I think he was a bit shocked, but I couldn't blame him, after what he had been through.

John was in hospital for over three weeks, and once it was nearing the time to go home, I started to think about transport. There were notices all around the ward, saying that transport wouldn't be provided, but we lived over seventy miles from Nottingham. When I made enquiries and explained that we had no means of getting home, because we were brought from Boston by hospital car, I was told that even if transport were provided for John, I wouldn't be allowed to join him. Eventually we had to book a taxi, and that cost us over £100.

It was a very tiring journey for John, but it was lovely to have him home. He couldn't wait to see his garden. I had paid someone to plant all his runner beans in the garden, transplanting them from the little fibre pots he'd planted them in before going to hospital. There were about four hundred plants. He used to sell runner beans outside the bungalow when he harvested them, and got so excited when people bought them. He didn't make a lot of money, but it gave him a purpose in life, and he said it paid for his seeds.

Before John left hospital, Mr Beggs, told him that he was going to refer him to an oncologist, Dr Bessel. He was a bit surprised after what the doctor in Boston had said to him. When we attended the appointment on 22 August, we waited for over two hours to see him. Dr Bessell said that ideally he should have had chemotherapy before the operation, but he understood that the oncologist in Boston wouldn't give it to him.

Dr Bessell suggested that John have six eight-hour treatments at three weekly intervals. The first one was on 17 September. First of all we had to go to a group meeting of people who were going to have treatment. I found it very upsetting. I sat with him all day, and didn't think much of the nursing staff, who just put the drip up and left him. No one offered him a drink or anything to eat. I felt like he was just a number; a bit like being on a conveyer belt. We stayed in the patient hotel for the night, and had a meal at the restaurant. John didn't have much, and was very ill during the night and spent most of the time on the toilet.

The next week was hell! He wasn't eating and he had a large cocktail of tablets to take. I said, "John, you're taking all those tablets and you haven't got any food inside you." He didn't know what to say. He was just doing what the doctor had told him to do.

After a week, I rang the surgery and asked for a doctor to call, and he could see that John was very dehydrated. He told him to drink plenty of liquid. John told him that he didn't want to go back into hospital, but when I was showing him out, the doctor said, "I'll come again tomorrow and if he's no better, he'll have to go into hospital," and that is what happened. He was put on a saline drip and was in hospital for over two weeks. He decided that he wouldn't have any more chemotherapy; it made him feel so awful.

He started to do little bits in the garden and garage again. I went down to the garage one day, he was sitting at his bench: an old grocery unit with lots of drawers and brass handles, which were black with age. I said, "Those handles would look great if they were cleaned!" I never thought any more about it. Then one day I went down to the garage again, and he had taken some of the handles off and was cleaning them. Another time I said that if the unit was rubbed down and re-varnished it would look lovely. He started to do that as well. Tears came to my eyes, because, as ill as he was, he was still doing things. He also kept his veg garden tidy. I did the watering when I could.

Chapter Twenty-Three

Another Christmas had passed. Trevor came, and John enjoyed seeing him opening his presents. We used to buy little things through the year, but we gave him money as his main present, or bought something for his home. Once again John ate very little; the weight was just falling off him; it was pitiful to see. We were into a new year and all we could do was to pray that he would improve.

It was 2008 and John's friend Jimmy was going to be sixty. He and his wife, Jennifer, had recently moved to Scotland. John wanted to pay him a surprise visit. I had a quiet word with Jennifer and she said that we could stay there, but as John wasn't very keen on staying with friends or relatives, we decided to stay for two nights in a hotel on the way up, two nights with Jimmy and Jennifer and two nights in a hotel on the way back. I didn't think that John was well enough to be going anywhere, but it wasn't until April, so I just hoped he would be feeling better. I booked the hotels, and Jennifer sent us the tickets for the ferry to get to where they lived. However, about a month before, John said to me, "I don't think I'll be able to go to Scotland; I don't feel well enough."

I said, "Don't worry, I'll cancel the bookings and let Jennifer know." He was very disappointed.

John had an appointment with Mr Beggs at our local hospital. When he told him that he was still experiencing a lot of pain, he said, "Of course you are. I've nearly cut you in half!" He didn't even examine him! He told him he would see him again in six months' time.

John was getting weaker by the day, but he still managed to do a few things. He spent a lot of time looking at the television. We bought a twenty-inch flat screen television for the bedroom. He got a lot of pleasure from looking at the teletex. He said there were always things on it that you didn't see on the news. After a few weeks, he was complaining that he couldn't see the teletex, and said he wanted a bigger television. We went into town, and he picked a thirty-seven inch screen. When I saw it, I said, "John, it's far too big." I told the assistant that it was only for the bedroom; he agreed with me that it was too big. John walked out of the shop in a huff.

About two weeks later, I was in the bedroom and he was again complaining that he couldn't see the teletex. So I said, "Come on let's go and buy your television." That cheered him up. I thought he hasn't got much in life at the moment, so I can't begrudge him this. He was very happy after that; like a child with a new toy!

After the August bank holiday, my friend Maureen, who lives at Bognor-Regis, came to stay for a week. She got a train to Victoria Station in London, then the coach to Boston, where I met her. Before we got home, I warned her that she would notice the change in John. She later thanked me for preparing her. She said I couldn't believe it was him; he had been such a big man.

There was a steam fair nearby, so I decided to go with Maureen. I asked John if he would like to come, but he said, "No, I'd like to, but I think I should stay here." It was a lovely day, and there was a lot to see. As we were walking around, we stopped to admire a Goldwing motorbike, and the owner asked Maureen if she would like to sit on it, but she refused. I wanted to though! I had quite a job to get on because of the restricted movement in my knees. I have about forty photos of that day, which included one of me on the motorbike.

When we got home, I showed John the photos I had taken, and he said, "I wish I'd come with you now."

I said," I don't think you would have coped with the walking." The ground was very uneven, and he was still on crutches. He had a good laugh about me getting on the motorbike.

When I told Trevor, he said, "Mum, you don't even like motorbikes."

Maureen with clown.

Veronica

On the Saturday, I decided to take Maureen to the designer clothes shop, Boundary Mills at Grantham. It is about forty miles away, and I had never driven there before, but I knew where it was and I felt confident about driving there. The night before, I asked John if he would like to come with us. He said, "Yes, but only if I can do the driving," so I agreed. I made sandwiches and coffee for a snack lunch, as we had booked to go out in the evening. Maureen couldn't believe that John drove all that way. I never felt nervous when he was driving; he was a very good driver. It was good to be with Maureen for those few days. We had been friends since 1955, and I didn't know when I would see her again.

A letter arrived one day from Bridlington, and I knew what it was before I opened it. It was from the hotel about the 'Gold Card Weekend.' The date was for the beginning of November. I told John, and said, "We won't be able to go. You're not well enough."

He said, "If you can get the suite, we'll go."

I rang the hotel, and managed to get booked. I thought if he wasn't well enough when the time came, I would cancel, and we would only lose the deposit.

We managed to go to Bridlington. I will never know how John did the driving! We met up with our friends, and it was good to be back at the hotel. The food and company were excellent. John was very weak by this time. After breakfast, we would go for a little drive and then go back to the hotel. John would go to bed with two hot water bottles, and I would go for a walk or sit in the lounge and have a read. John was eating very little, and most days just had a starter and a dessert. I knew in my heart that we were only there for my benefit.

The next few weeks, John spent a lot of time in bed. I couldn't even hug him, because he was too frail. Once when I sat on the bed, he said, "I feel terrible."

I said, "I wish I could help you!"

He replied, "You're doing all you can."

It was nearly Christmas, and Trevor would be coming once again. We always asked him what he would like for dinner. Normally he would say, "I don't mind, Mum." But this year he said, "How about a goose?"

I said, "All right, but I've never cooked a goose, and I've heard people say that they are very fatty." I went to our butchers and ordered one. The butcher told me that they were very expensive. He asked me what size. I told him it was for three people. I knew John wouldn't eat very much, so I settled on a small one.

I arranged to pick it up on Christmas Eve, and when the butcher put the box with the goose on the counter, I asked how much it was, nearly falling through the floor when he replied, "Forty-three pounds."

The goose was a great success. I got lots of goose dripping and stock, and it wasn't a bit fatty. John even managed to eat a little. We didn't tell Trevor how much it cost until after dinner. He said, "Mum, I told you not to buy one, because I knew they were expensive." We were all pleased that the meal was worth it. It even had instructions how to cook it, and I made the stuffing from a recipe in a little book that was in the box.

Trevor opened his presents, but his main present was money. I gave him a cheque at the dinner table and after dinner, John said to me, "Shall we buy him a television?" knowing that his had packed up. John then tore the cheque up, and told Trevor to choose whatever television he wanted and we would pay for it over the phone. Trevor was a bit shocked but John had obviously been thinking about it. That was the kind of thing he would do.

The weekend after Trevor went home, John's ankles became very swollen. I told him I was going to phone the doctor on the Monday morning. He didn't want me to, but I had no choice. The doctor was a bit concerned about John's chest. He asked me if I could get him to the hospital for an x-ray? I said I could and took him the next day. He had the x-ray then was asked to go in for another one. The doctor said that he was going to fax the results through to the GP, and when John asked what was wrong, he was told, "You've got some fluid on your lung."

I rang the doctor the next day, and he said he hadn't had a fax from the hospital, but he would make enquiries and ring me back, which he did, and told me a doctor would call that day, which was New Year's Eve. While I was waiting for the doctor, I rang BUPA to see what the position was about John going into the private wing of our hospital; I was told that he had to be admitted by a consultant.

Dr Latchem, who was our usual doctor, came and told John that he would have to go into hospital to have the fluid drained off his lung. I told him that I wanted him to go into the private wing, but he had to be admitted by a consultant. He rang the Bostonian (the private wing of our hospital) and spoke to a Dr Mangeon, who agreed to admit him. John and I knew him, so that was good news. I had to take him there. When we got to the hospital, we had to wait for a room to be ready. When we eventually got taken to room 12a, the first thing that John said was, "This used to be number 13!" He was very superstitious. He got settled in, and I waited until early evening, then I went home.

Chapter Twenty-Four

2009 did not start very well for us; in fact we hadn't had a good New Year for quite a while, but this was the worst one yet. I spent most of my time at the hospital, sometimes even having my meals there. Because John was hardly eating any food, the chef very kindly gave me mine for free.

The doctor inserted a tube into John's lung to drain the fluid, and he had to have it done several times, because when the doctor tried to take it out, air got in. It was very distressing for John, and also for me having to watch.

Over a few weeks, I was getting one cold after another, and because of this I didn't sit too near John, because I didn't want him to catch anything. I have always regretted that, but I was just thinking of him. I used to go to the day room part of the time, so that he could have a rest. One day a nurse came to talk to me, and I broke down under all the pressure. She said to me, "You know, a lot of people would like to have what you and your husband have got."

John got on really well with the nurses. One day I said to him, "You've always been a ladies' man."

He replied, "Have I?", but he knew very well what I meant.

I had a phone call from Irene, to say that she and Ernie would like to visit John. Ernie is the man who John made friends with at Nottingham. The day they chose was a good one, because I had an appointment somewhere. The day before, I told him that I wouldn't be in until the afternoon. I didn't tell him about Irene and Ernie visiting. After they had been to visit John, they came to see me. It was a lovely surprise. Irene told me that John had had a fall, and he had asked her not to tell me, but she thought I should know. When I went to visit, I could see that his arm was bandaged. I said, "What have you done to your arm?"

He said, "I had a fall. It's nothing. That was cheeky not telling me that Ernie and Irene were coming to visit me!"

It was a lot of bandage for nothing. After that, he was told that he mustn't get out of bed on his own, and the nurses had to put the sides of his bed up.

That Saturday, Jennifer and Jimmy came down from Scotland to visit him. I had rung them to let them know how ill John was. They had a shock when they saw him. I hadn't told him that they were coming. John was so pleased to see them. When it was time to leave, Jimmy got quite emotional. I walked out of the room with them, and I could see how choked up Jimmy was. I had never thought of him as a softy; not like John. You could see the sorrow in his eyes. He and John had been friends for a very long time.

At the beginning of the next week, I had a phone call from the ward sister early in the morning. The first thing that I thought was that John had died. She said, "John's had another fall, he's cut his head." I felt sick! I told her I would be there soon. When I got to the hospital and saw him, I nearly passed out. A doctor came in and tried to stitch his head; it was terrible. He couldn't stitch it, so ended up trying to pull the wound together and then put a plaster on it.

About half an hour later, the doctor returned bringing another doctor with him. One of them said, "We're going to try and staple it." I couldn't believe it, but they did it. Later in the day his doctor sent him for a brain scan. He had a bleed on the brain. I wasn't very happy about the whole thing, because after the first fall he shouldn't have been able to get out of bed. The sides should have been pulled up.

One day when I went in and the sides were down, I said, "John who left the sides down?"

He said, "You did."

I said, "No I didn't, I've only just come in."

Arrangements were being made for him to come home. A nurse was going to come in at night. A bed was delivered, which had to be put in our lounge, because there was nowhere else for it to go. John said, "I'm coming home to die, aren't I?"

I said, "John, how can I answer that?"

Another day when I went in, the sides of the bed were down and his bed hadn't been made, so I gave him a wash. He wouldn't let the nurses wash him. He used say to them that his wife would do it. After I had washed him, I went and told the nurses that they could make his bed now. Three of them came into the room, and I said, "By the way, the sides of the bed were down again." They were all very quiet, and didn't say a thing.

The doctor came to see John while I was there. He said, "I think we should do a swallow (an x-ray after swallowing some special liquid). We have been concentrating on your lung, but I think we should check your stomach." I got a bit upset, because I didn't think he could cope with it.

On the Thursday, Beth and Frank visited him. I think they were very shocked to see how he had deteriorated. That evening after they had gone, the doctor came with the results of the test. He said, "I'm afraid the cancer is back where it was originally."

John was very upset and he said, "Doctor, please, give me something, or I will go to Switzerland." He wouldn't have gone anyway, because he wouldn't fly.

I said, "The doctor can't do that darling."

He said, "I can give him some diamorphine."

John agreed to the treatment. A bit later a nurse came in and put a little box on his stomach. John said, "This is it, isn't it?" She didn't answer. He remembered that his mum had diamorphine when she was very ill.

A bit later on, he rang Trevor, to say goodbye, and to tell him that he loved him. I could hear him sobbing, so I took the phone off John, and told him to put the phone down compose himself and ring back later, and that is what he did. John asked me if there was anything that I wanted to say to him. I said, "Only that I love you, and I don't want you to go."

He said, "I do love Linda!"

I said, "I know, but it is too late now.

He said, "I'm dreading you going home!"

I asked him if he would like me to stay. He said, "No."

When I went in the next day, I met the doctor before going into the room, who said, "He's a lot brighter today. I can arrange for him to have a stent put down, to enable him to eat."

I said, "No, I think he's suffered enough, doctor."

He replied, "I can increase the diamorphine."

I went into his room, he seemed a bit better, but he was a bit delirious.

One of the nurses told me that John had upset some of the young nurses by saying goodbye to them.

Our friends, Paddy and Edna, were coming to see him. Again, I didn't tell him they were coming. He was pleased to see them, but he slept some of the time, so we went to the day room for a drink. John had been friendly with Paddy for a long time. When we went back into the room, he was a bit delirious. He was seeing things that weren't there. When I went out of the room with Paddy and Edna as they were going home, I told them that I was going to stay the night.

When the night staff came on duty, the staff nurse, Carol, came into see John. She was trying to keep him still, because his arms and legs were all over the place. She was kissing his forehead, and she said, "This is what makes my job worthwhile. I shouldn't be doing this with Mrs McBean sitting there."

John said, "It's Veronica."

She got him settled, and then said to me, "Now then, what are you going to do?"

I said, "I'm not going home."

She left the room. A bit later she came back in the room, and took hold of my hand. She said, "Come with me," and took me to another room.

She said, "This bed is empty, I'll call you if anything happens." I did get a few hours' sleep.

The next morning, I was up very early, and had a wash in John's bathroom. The housekeeper brought me some tea and toast. Everyone was so kind. Trevor was going to be coming later in the day. John had hardly moved since the night before. I went and got a newspaper, but found it hard to concentrate.

When Trevor arrived in the afternoon, I decided to go home for a shower. John hadn't opened his eyes all day. I wasn't gone for more than an hour, and when I got back the nurse was checking his pulse. I said, "Has he gone?"

He said, "I need to get another nurse to confirm."

I think he had already died before I went home, because when the nurse tried to close his mouth, he couldn't; it was set. A nurse hadn't come in the room for some time. The second nurse confirmed he had died. She later came back and put a flower on his pillow; he would have loved that. He loved flowers. I thought it was a lovely thing to do. Trevor went out of the room and left me to say goodbye.

We had to wait in the day room for the doctor to sign the death certificate. The sister said that we could collect his personal belongings the next day. I didn't drive home. Trevor took me in his car, and we collected mine the next day. The weather was terrible; we had had a lot of snow. When we got home, I had a phone call from Carol, the staff nurse. She said, "I went straight in to see John when I came on duty. I couldn't believe that he had gone so soon. He was a lovely man."

I said to Trevor, "We won't make any phone calls until tomorrow." It left a big hole in my life; we were really going to miss him. Life would never be the same again.

Conclusion

I chose to end my story with John's death, but of course in the years since then life has gone on, as life does. Just because your world falls apart, it doesn't mean that everything stops.

Amid all the sadness and loss, I am very grateful. I am grateful for friends and family who have come and gone over the years and left their mark. So many have been very kind and loving. I am also grateful for all the kindness and expertise of the medical staff who treated us in the various hospitals. Above all, I am grateful that I have had the experience of living with two very loving husbands. They each had different characters, but both gave me so much love and support as we journeyed through our lives together.

Readers may wonder if there has been a reconciliation with Linda, but to date that has not happened. I have seen her twice since the breakdown of our relationship: once at a friend's funeral, and in May 2022, when a plaque was put up outside the fire station where Dave had worked.

I wrote again to her after my friend's funeral telling her that I loved her and would never stop loving her, but I didn't get a reply. She has four children: three girls and a boy who is called David. I have talked to him, explaining that I had to choose between my family and my husband, and have invited him to visit if he wants to.

My main purpose in writing this book was to set myself a retirement challenge, and to give an account of my life that would be useful to future generations in my family. As I have written it, I have also become aware that I have described life from the war years through to modern times, and I believe it will be of interest to a wider audience.

Printed in Great Britain
by Amazon

22204677R00185